"The Original Bullshipper Gang"
Created by Thomas Brekke
for The Bullshipper, Walt Gabelmann
(1976 – 1981)

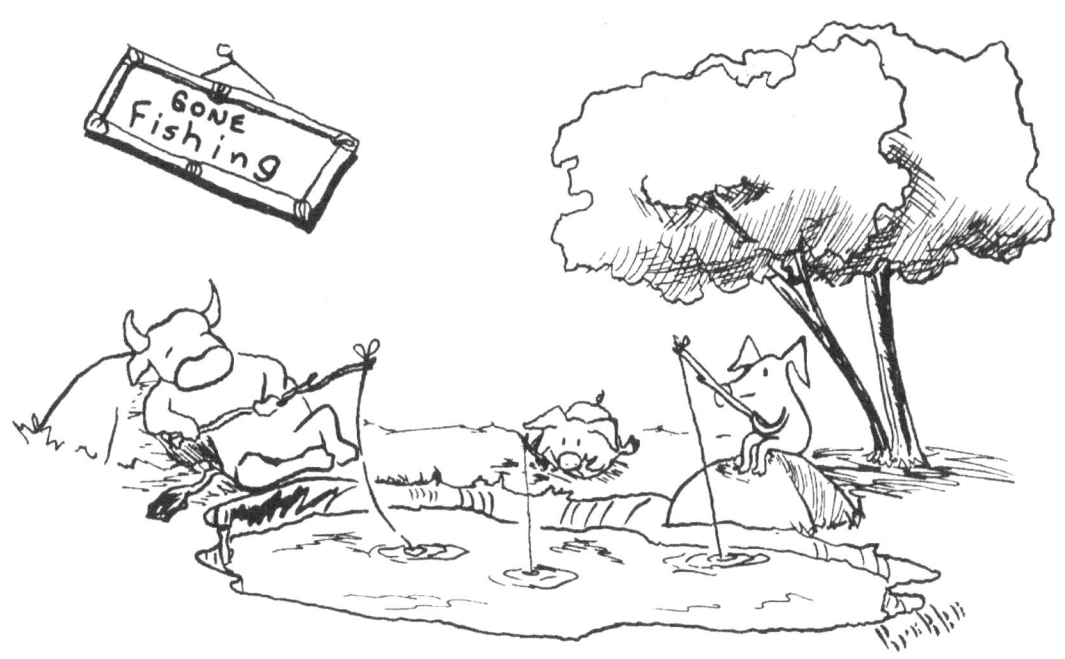

Illustrated by: Thomas Brekke
Contributions by: Ruthann Brekke, Matthew Brekke, and Jason Gansen

Dedications

Ruthann Brekke: I dedicate this book to the loving memory of my father, Walt Gabelmann, the Original Bullshipper. He was a kind man and through his love for others and service to his community, created a legacy in his family that will carry on for generations. I also dedicate this to my sons, Jason, Jeremy & Jeffrey Gansen. They were my dad's pride and joy and are very fine young men today because of him.

As Walt's son-in-law and Tom's brother, I also want to thank my husband, Frank Brekke, for his love and support.

Dad passed away from cancer in 2008, but his memory lives on. He will always be known as "The Bullshipper."

Matthew Brekke: I dedicate this book in memory of my father, Thomas Brekke, who illustrated these cartoons. Tom passed away from cancer in 2007. I felt the need to share his talents with others.

I also dedicate this book to my mother Sherri Brekke and all of dad's siblings: Ann, Frank, Michelle, Patricia, Katherine, Barbara, and Kristine who continue to be supportive to my family and me.

Jason Gansen: I dedicate this book in memory of my grandpa, Walt, who was always there for us and taught my brothers and me how to be, in his words, "fine young gentlemen."

I want to thank my mom, Ruthann, for her continuing support and unconditional love.

I also want to thank my loving wife, who was willing to let me follow my dreams of becoming an author and publisher. None of this could have been possible without her.

Forward

Written by Ruthann Brekke

Walt Gabelmann became the manager of the Riceville Sale Pavilion in 1959 at the age of 37. He had been a cattle buyer since he was in his late teens and was well known in northern Iowa and southern Minnesota.

Every week he wrote the livestock markets for the local paper, The Riceville Recorder. In the late 1970s, he hired Tom Brekke to spruce up his markets with cartoons. Tom created the Bullshipper Gang cartoon characters. Each week Tom would draw a cartoon, most times depicting the time of year and sometimes, local happenings. Some of his drawings show the mayor of the Bullshipper Gang's town, which was also Walt since he was on the city council and mayor of Riceville for 22 years total.

Tom passed away from colo-rectal cancer in 2007 and Walt passed away from prostate cancer in 2008. They had long since stopped the Bullshipper Gang cartoons, but the legacy of both of them lives on in these pages.

This book is a tribute to both men.

Tom's son Matt, Walt's daughter Ruthann and grandson Jason,
created this book to honor both of them.

Biographies

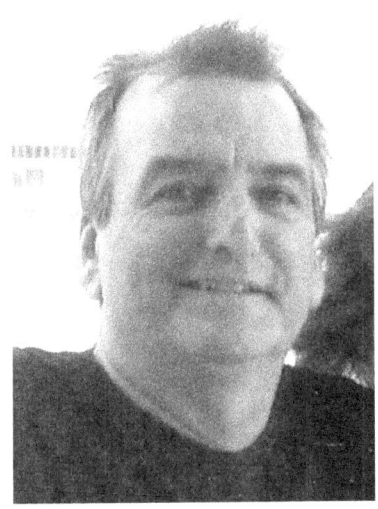

Thomas Brekke

March 1, 1952 - April 23, 2007

Thomas William Brekke was born March 1, 1952 to William and Lorraine Brekke. He was the 2nd oldest of 8 children and grew up on the family farm in Chester, Iowa.

Tom graduated from Riceville High School in 1970. He then joined the National Guard. He illustrated the Bullshipper Gang comic for the local paper. After working in farming and other odd jobs, including owning a bar, Tom met the love of his life, Sherri. They were married in August of 1985.

Tom and his wife moved to Winona, Minnesota in 1986 with their son Matthew. Tom graduated from Winona State University with a computer engineering degree. They moved to Lewiston, Minnesota in 1992. He worked for Candle Corporation and then for IBM.

Tom was a big part of the Lewiston community. He was a member of the Lions Club and founded the Legion baseball program in 1996.

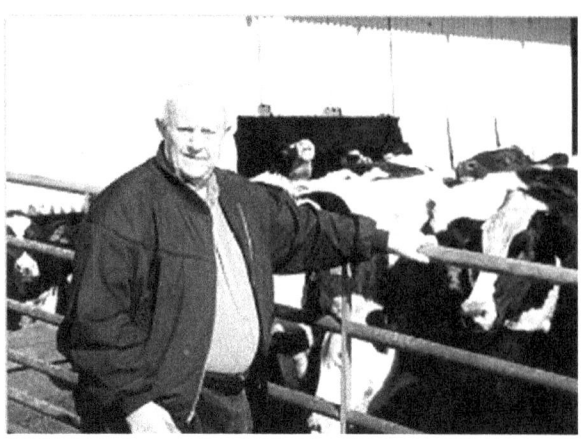

Walt Gabelmann
"The Original Bullshipper"
June 27, 1922 - December 14, 2008

Walt was born and raised on a farm near Charles City, Iowa on June 27, 1922. His dad, Christian Wilhelm Gabelmann, emigrated from Germany in 1883. Walt came to Riceville with his wife, Helene and daughter, Ruthann in 1959 to manage the Riceville Sale Pavilion, which he later purchased. After serving on the city council for 4 years, he became the mayor of Riceville from 1966-1984.

Some of Walt's accomplishments include:

- On committees in Riceville that created the golf course, library, paved streets, garbage system, the downtown gazebo/park area, nursing home, water tower, lagoon, and Lake Hendricks
- Member of the Iowa State Road Committee
- Member of the Howard County Fair Board
- Supporter of the Boy Scouts of America
- Donated his time and money to Dollars for Scholars
- Helped create the livestock-judging program at the Howard County Fair. He judged the competition and donated money to the kids that showed their animals
- Also known as the "Original Bullshipper" and "Pa" (by his family)

- Wrote "Bullshipping with Walt" in the Riceville Recorder for 48 years including the week he died
- Co-owner of WW Livestock, livestock buyer for the Cresco Sale Barn and Spring Valley Sale Barn.
- Sunday School teacher in Riceville
- Elder at a church in Nashua, IA and Deacon of United Church of Christ in Riceville, IA
- Industrial Development member
- President of the Community Betterment Program
- President of the Iowa Cattleman's Association
- President of the Riceville Community Club
- President of the Easter Egg Committee (he gave 30 dozen eggs to the rest home to color for the kids every year. Tom Brekke illustrated the Easter Egg coloring contest pictures)
- President of the Riceville Country Club
- President of the Riceville Kiwanis, a charter member
- Vice President and Co-founder of the Iowa/Minnesota Horse Association
- Honorary member of the Riceville National Honor Society
- Honorary chapter farmer of the FFA
- Received the Boy Scouts of America Eagles Award of Merit
- Century member of the Boy Scouts
- Sponsored and Bowled on teams for Riceville, Nashua, Greene, and Charles City
- 4-H Supporter and received the Honorary Award and Silver Sponsor Award
- Cavalcade of Sports member
- Master of Ceremonies for several of the Iowa Dairy, Pork, and Beef Association's banquets
- Sponsored the Dairy Princess for Howard and Mitchell counties

- At age 83 he was pictured and quoted in the September 2005 Smithsonian magazine
- He loved his community, state, and country. He loved donating to and helping people, special causes, and children.
- As he always said, he had friends "as many as the sands of the sea." Everyone knew Walt and everyone was his favorite. He often said, "You are only a stranger once to me."
- He was a master story and joke teller.
- He worked into his mid 80's and was still on some of the boards and committees he served until he passed away.

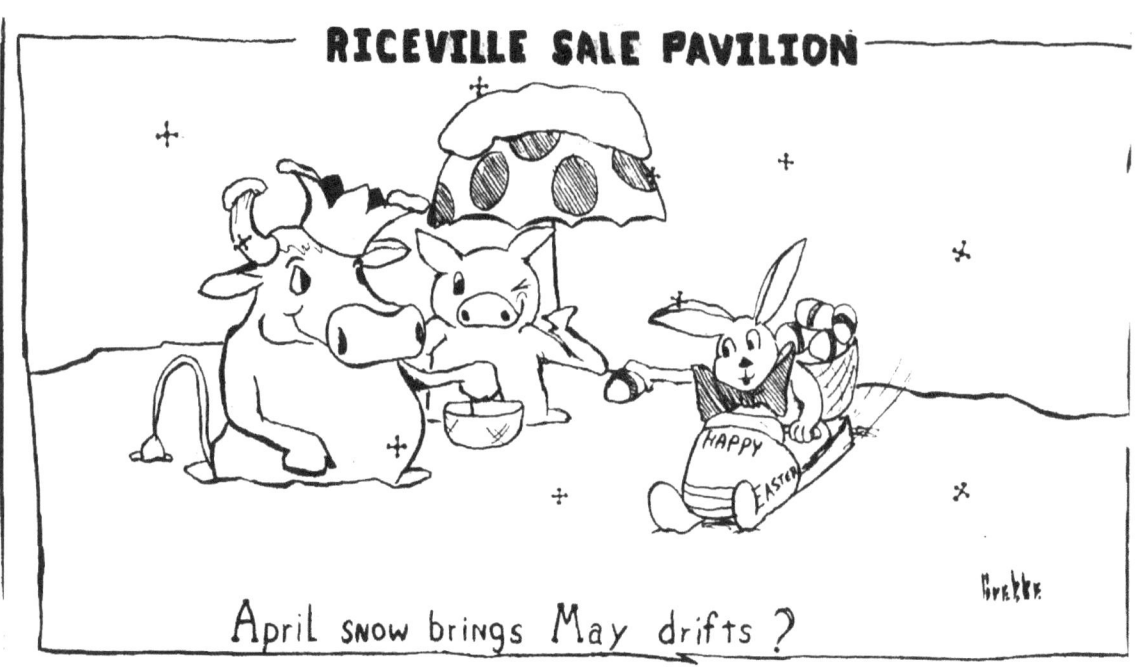

~ March 30 1976

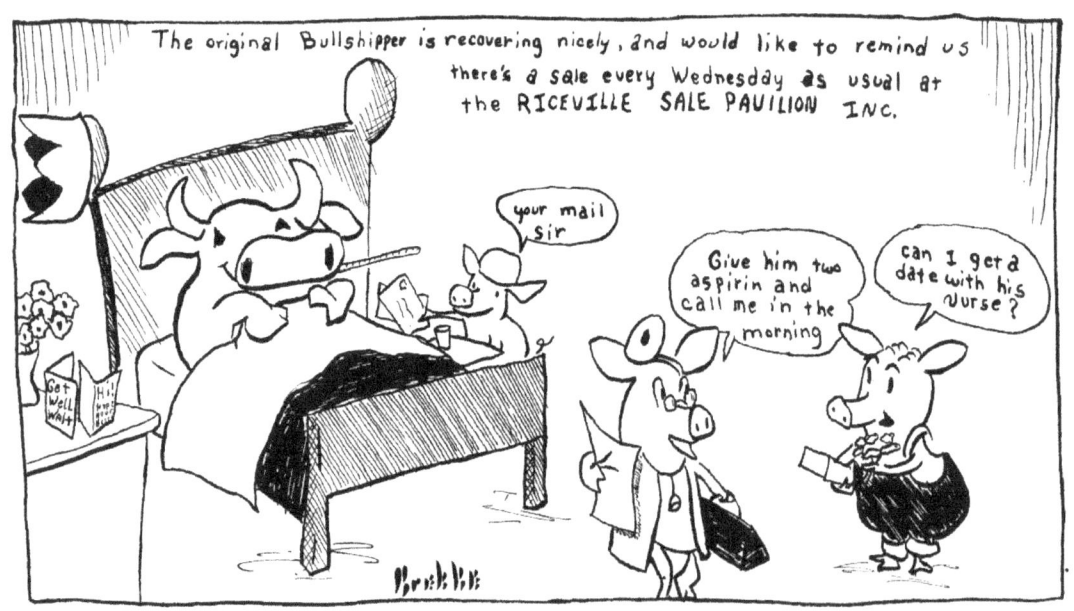

~ June 15, 22, 1976

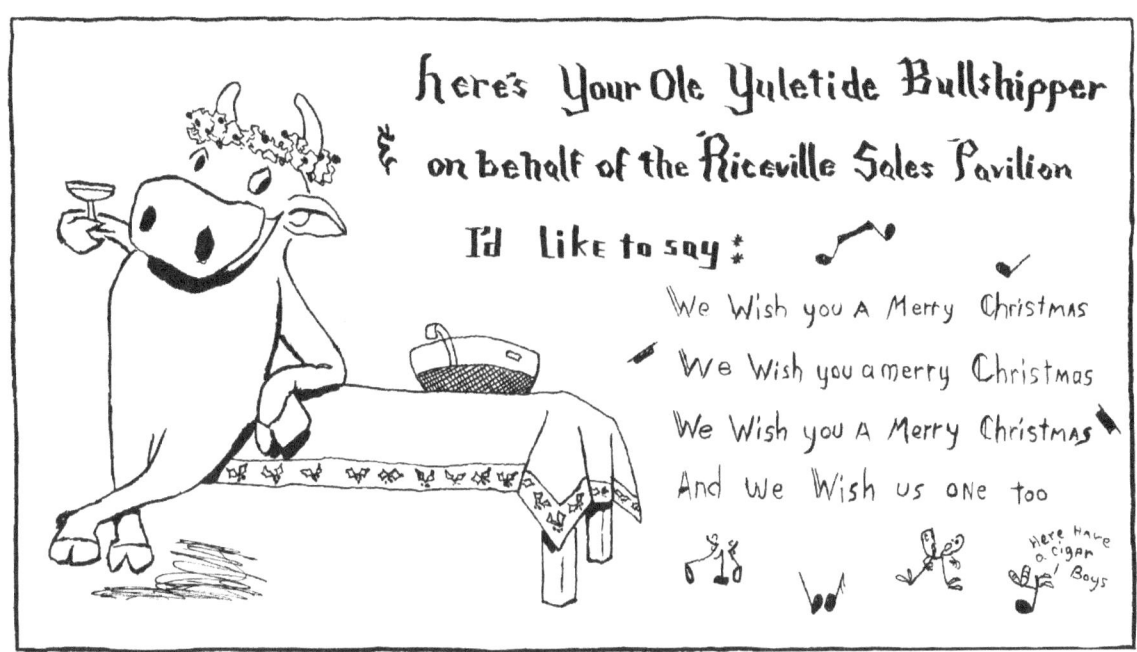

~ December 1, 1976

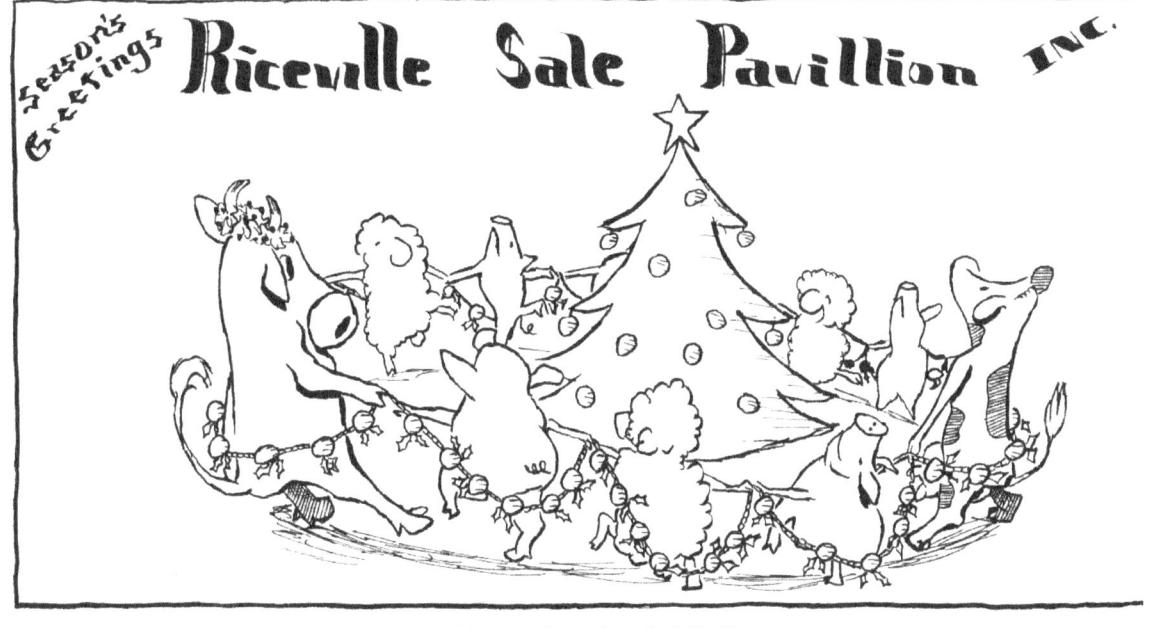

~ December 8, 15, 1976

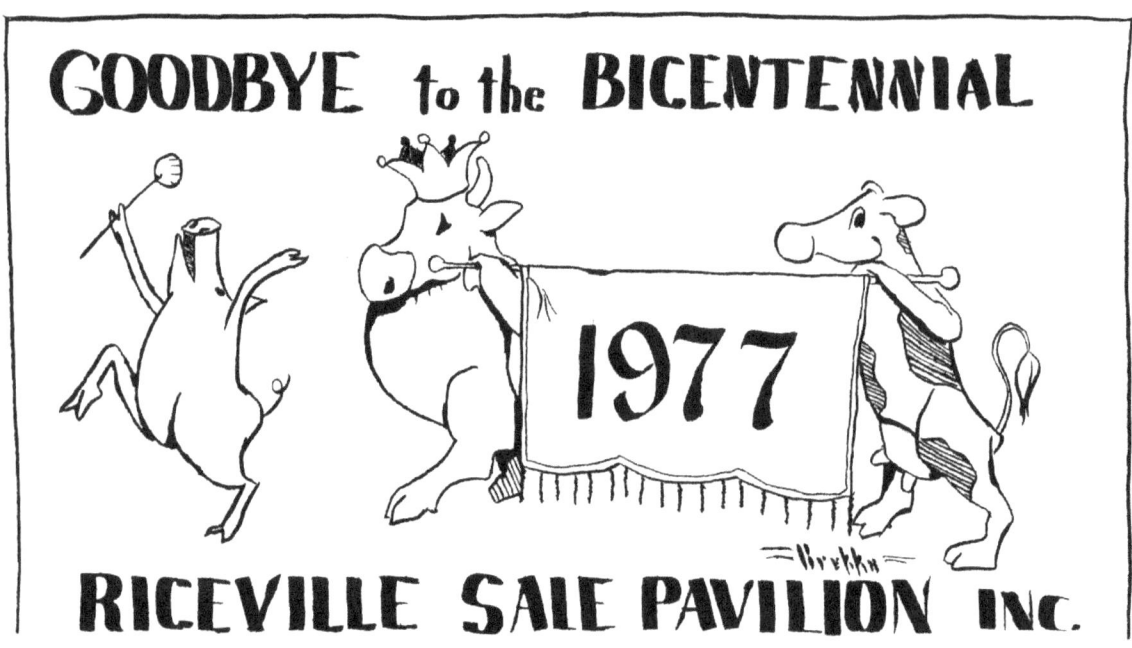

~ December 22, 1976

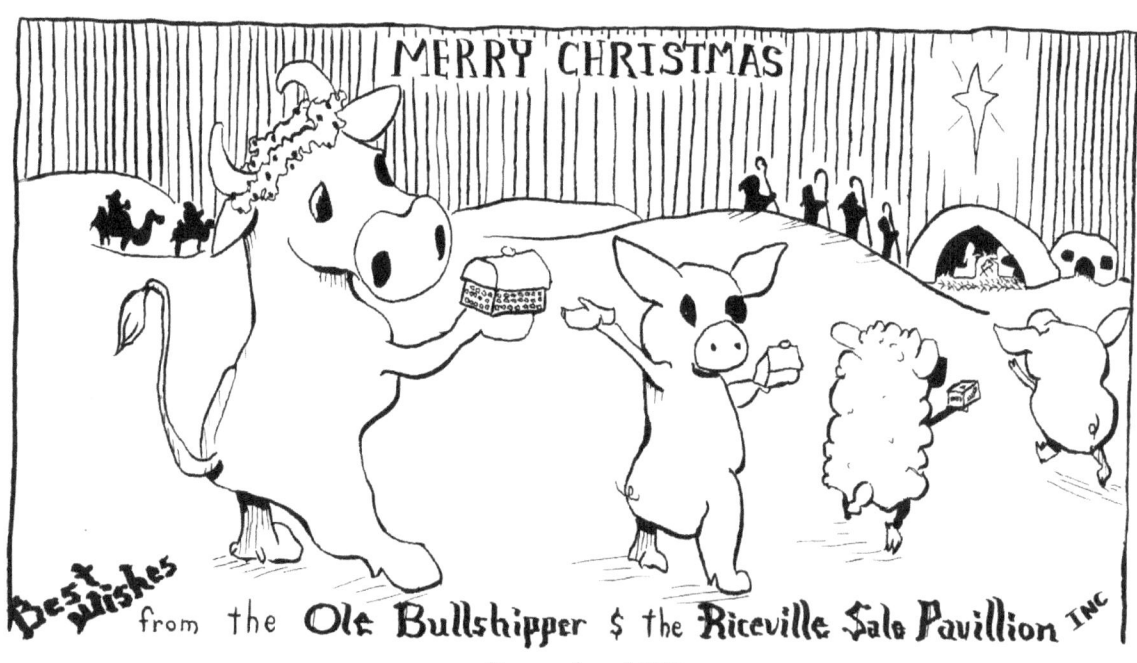

~ December 1976

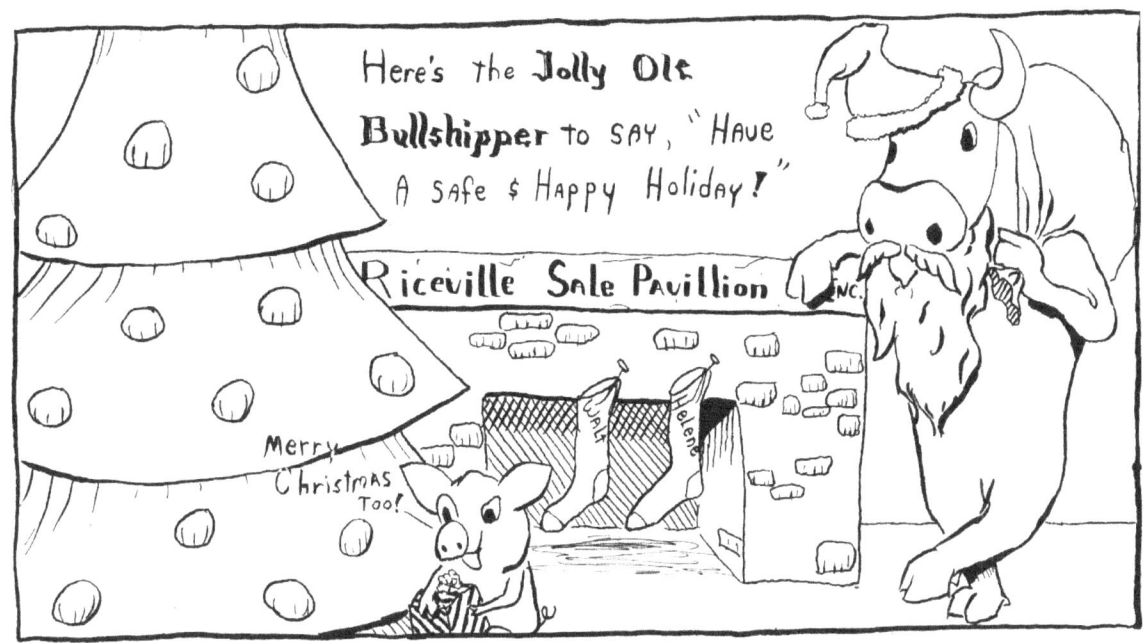

~ December 1976

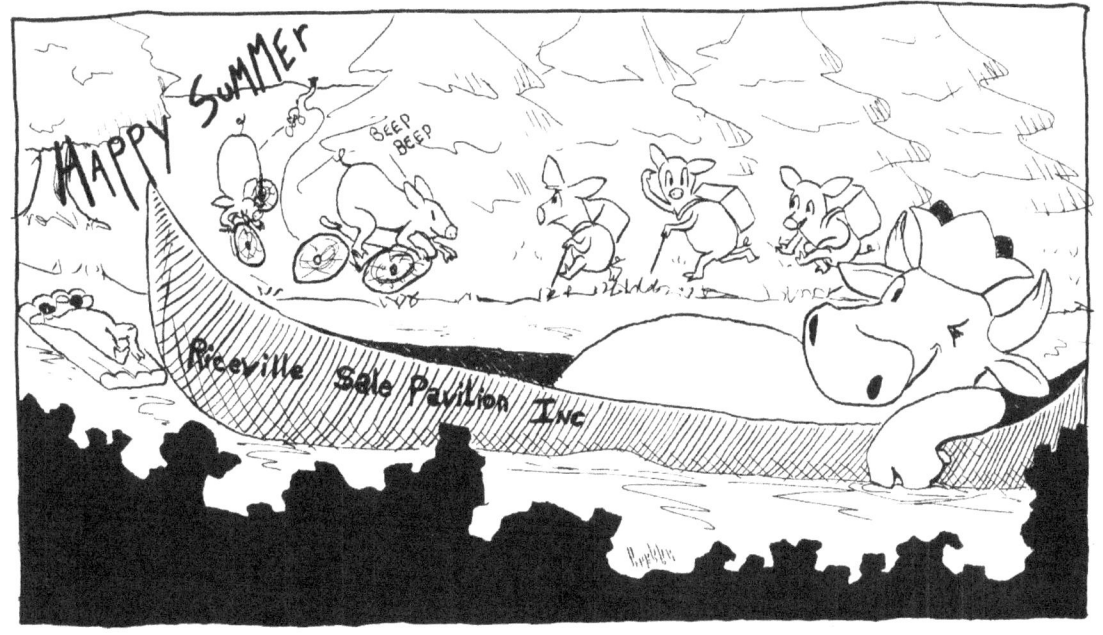

~ June 25, 1976

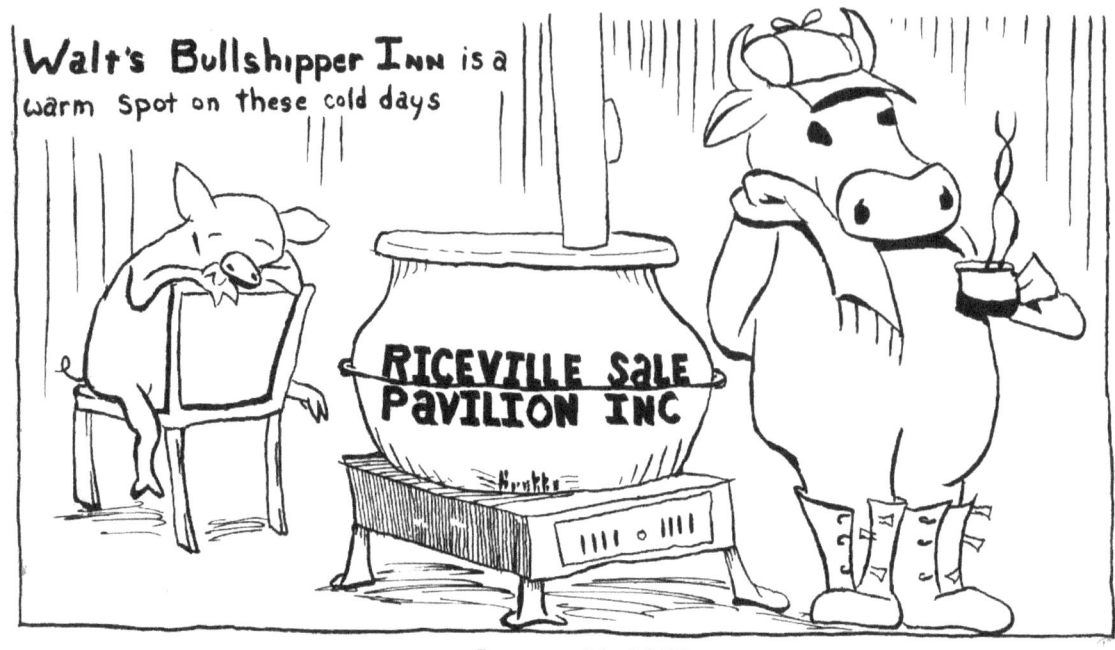

~ January 19, 1977

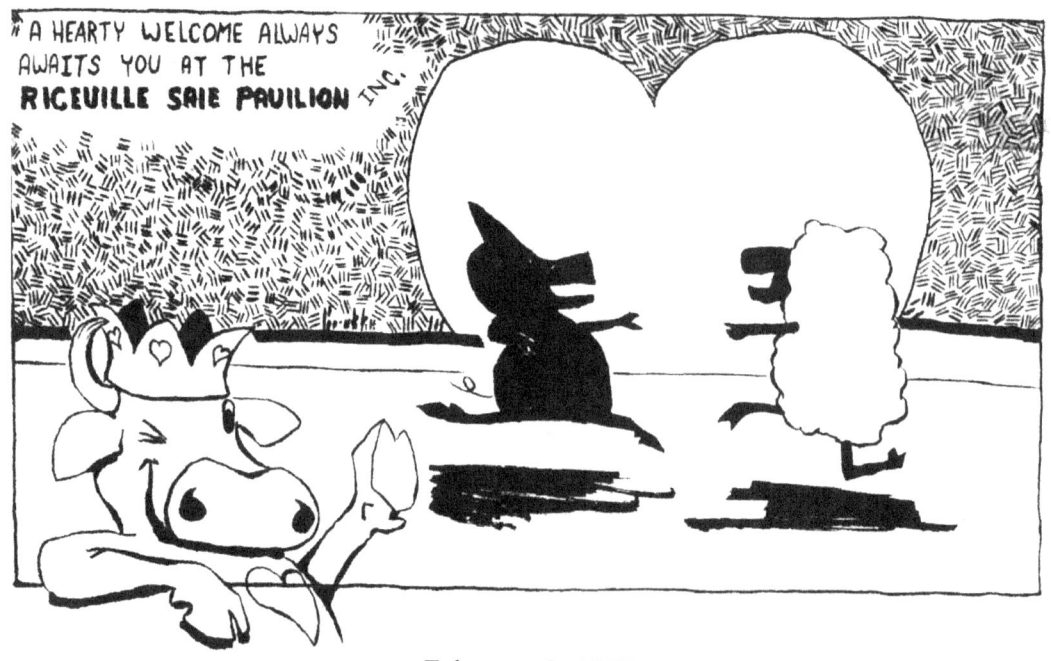

~ February 9, 1977

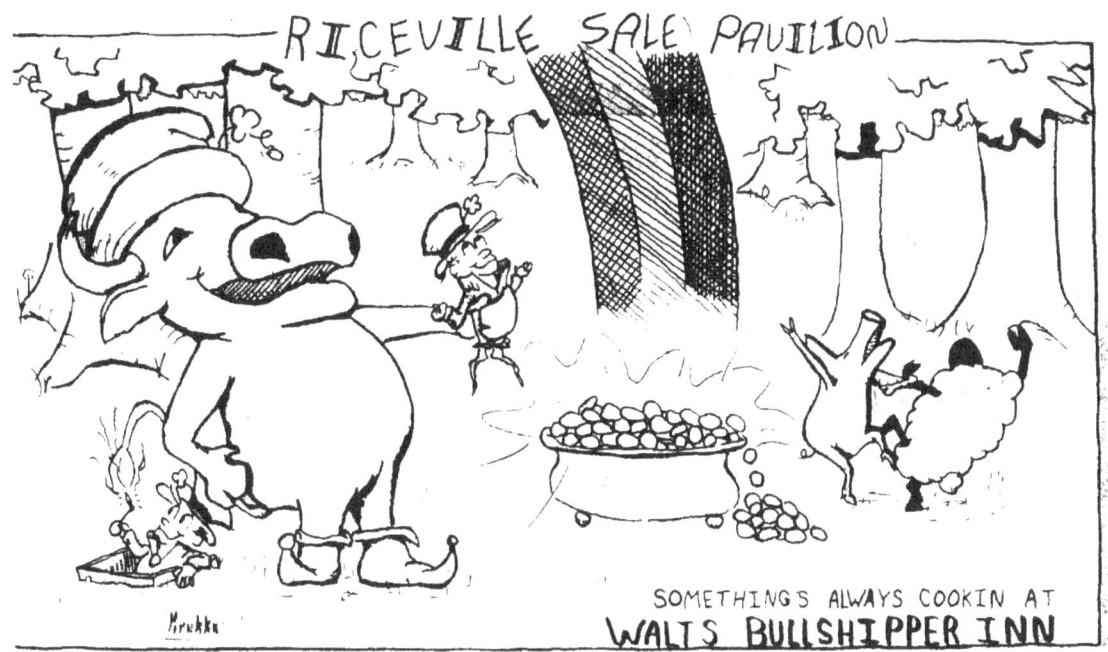

~ March 2, 16, 1977

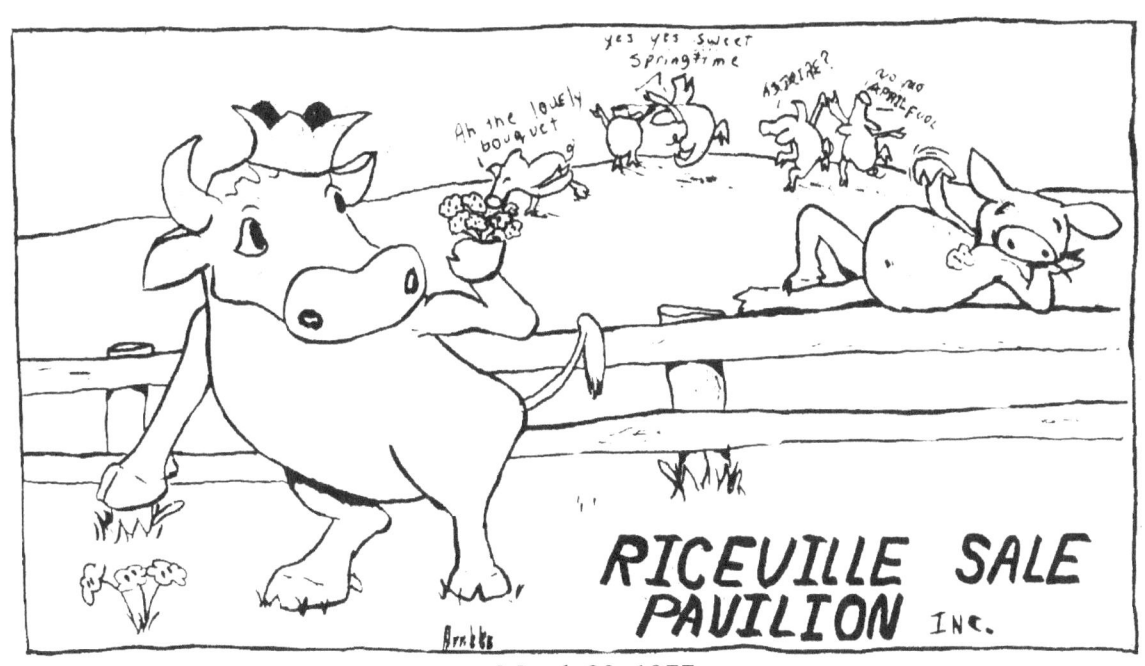

~ March 23, 1977

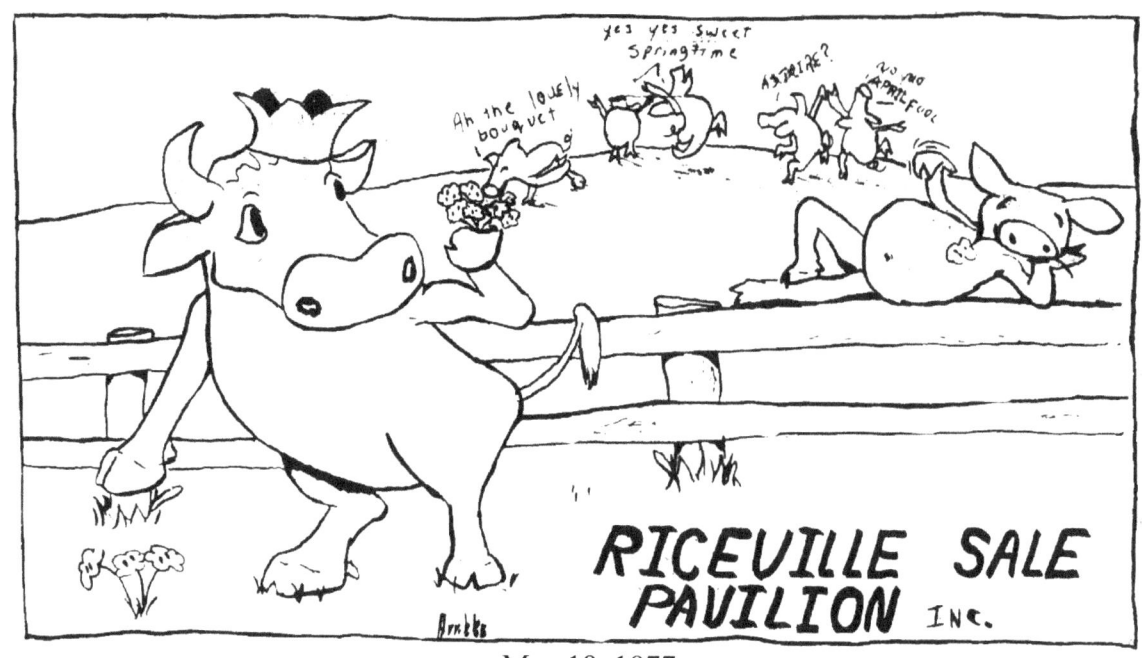

~ May 18, 1977

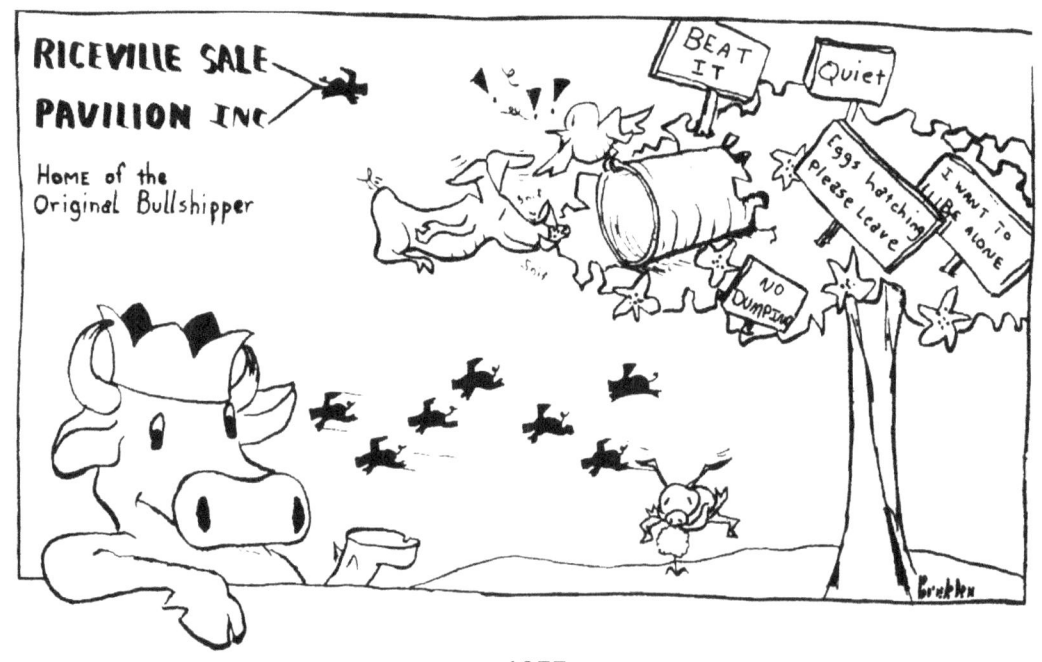

~ 1977

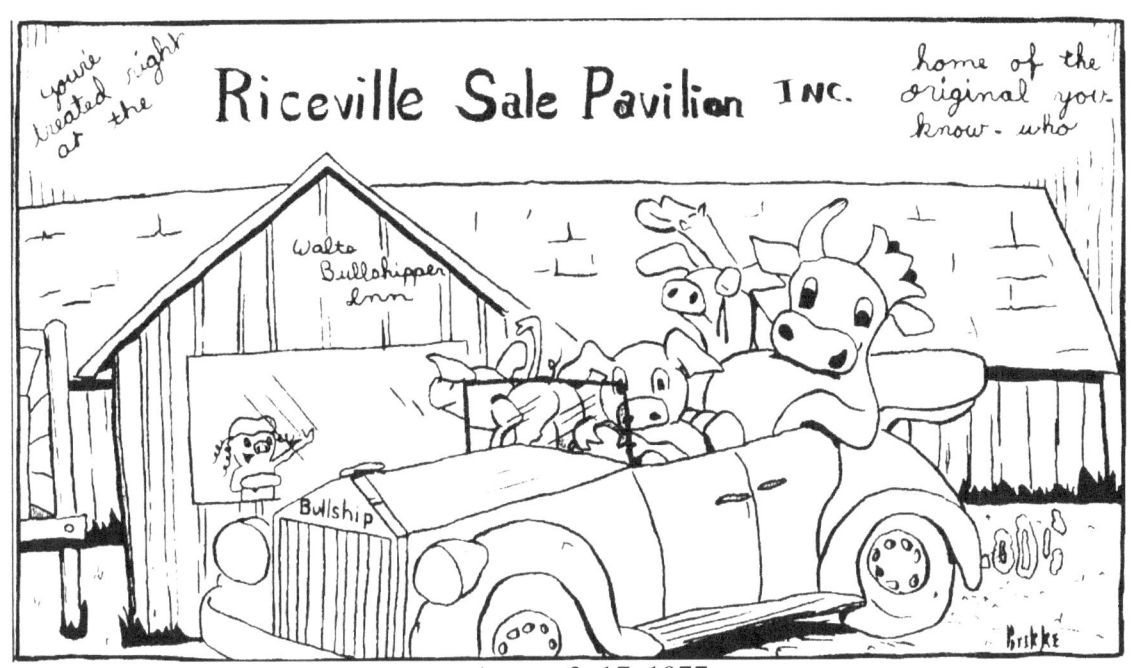

~ August 3, 17, 1977

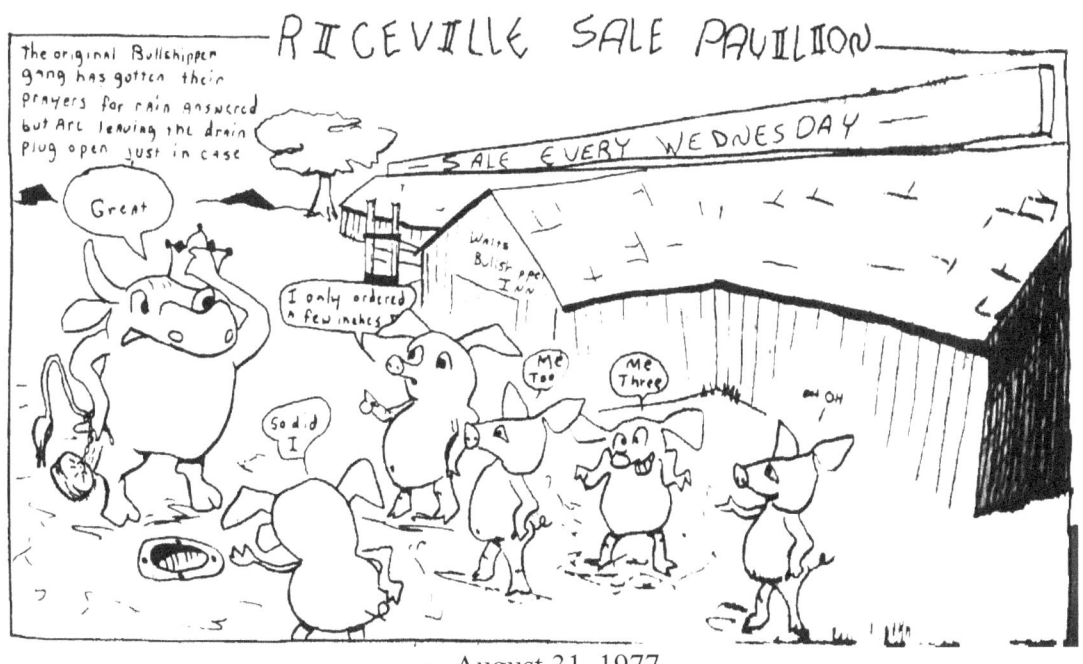

~ August 31, 1977

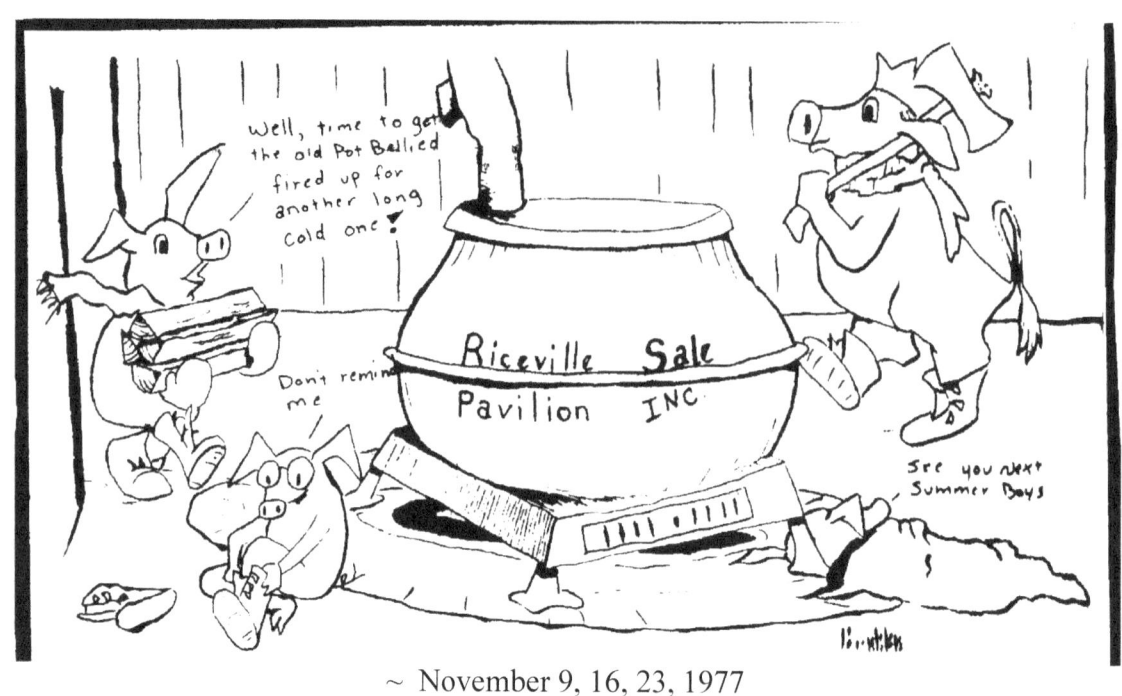

~ November 9, 16, 23, 1977

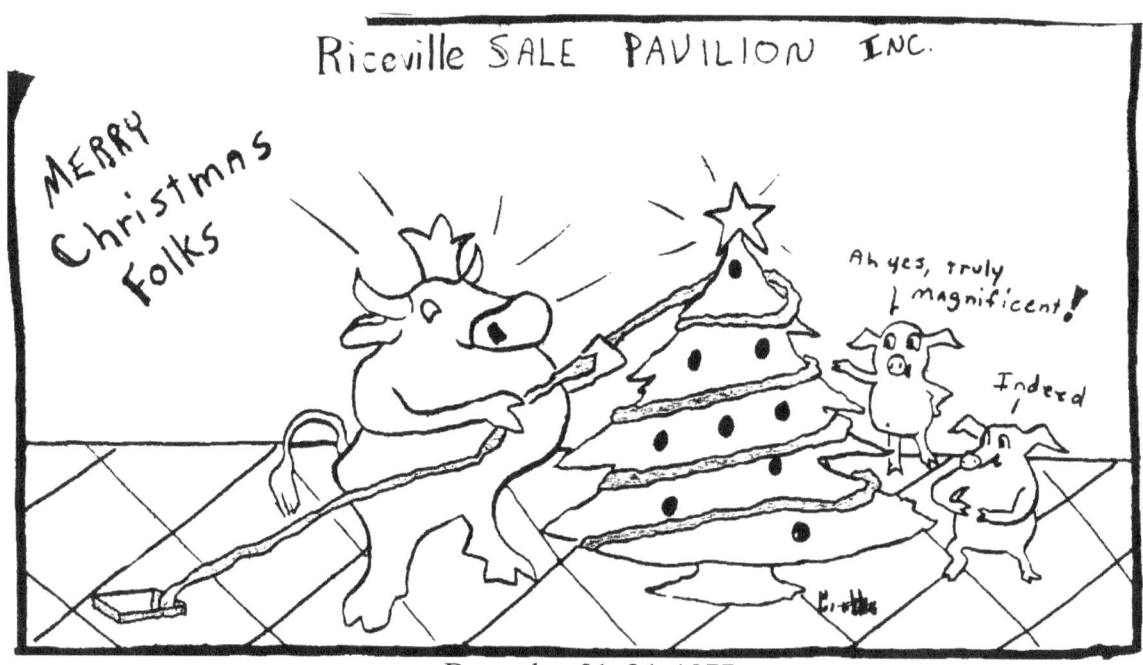

~ December 21, 24, 1977

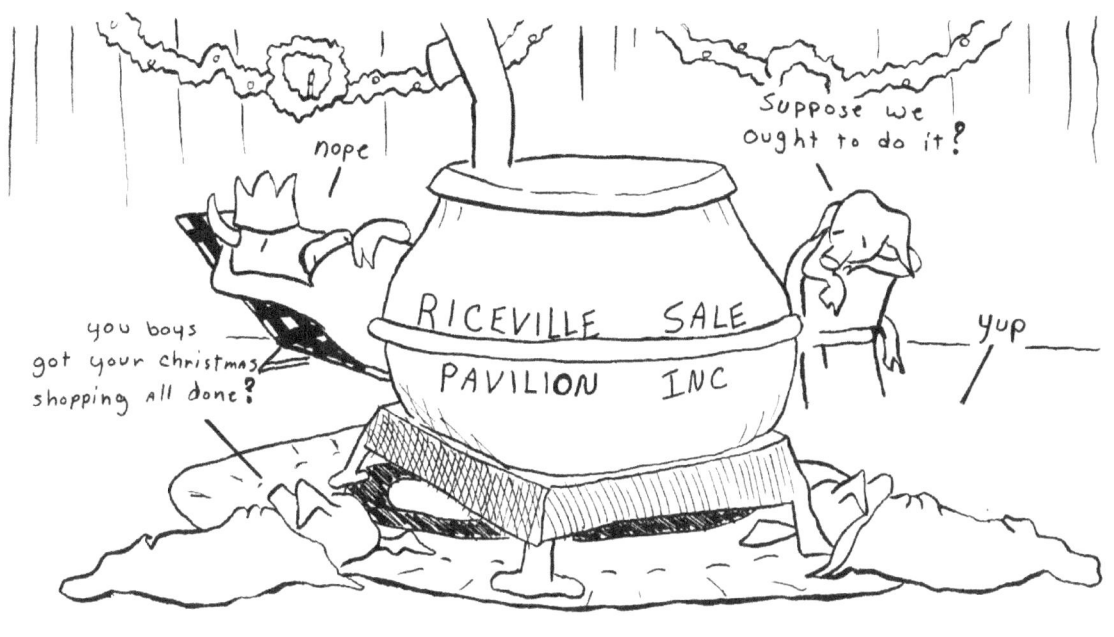

~ December 7, 1977

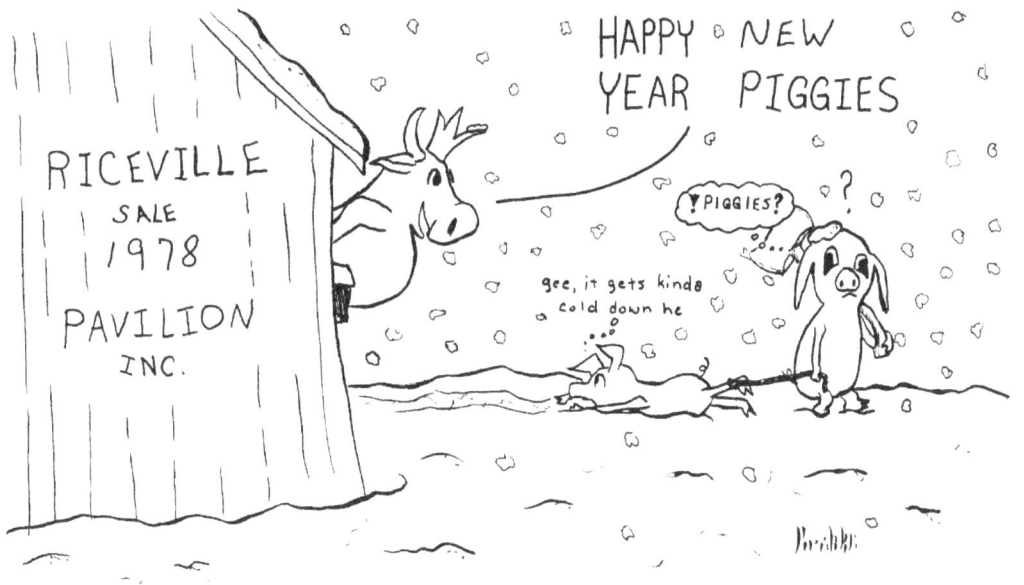

~ December 28, 1977 and January 4, 1978

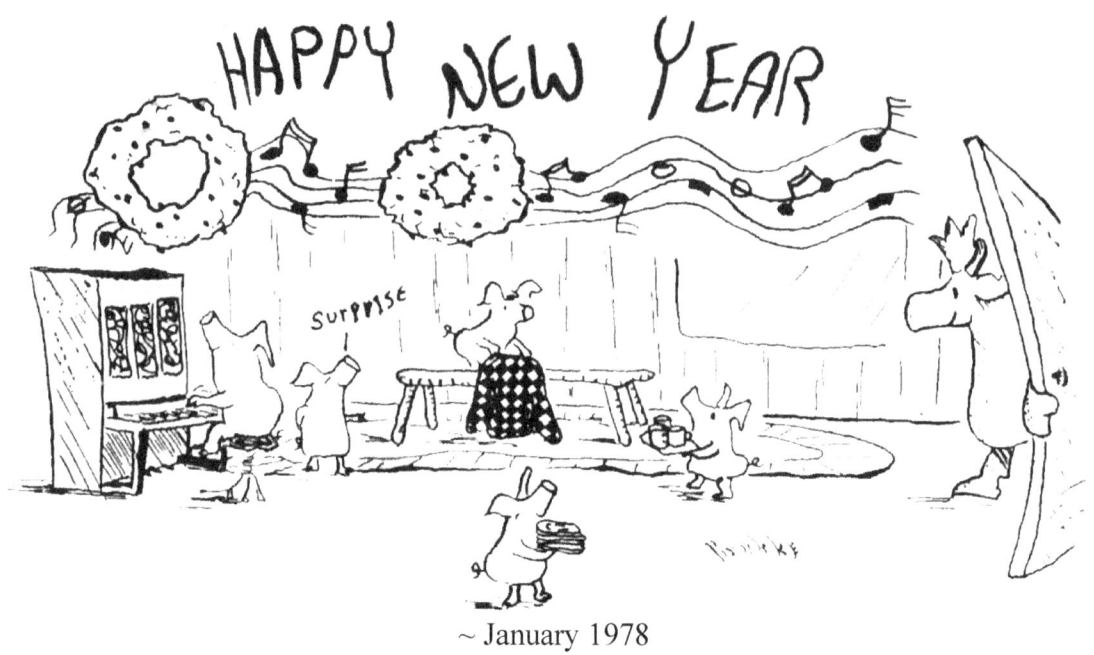

~ January 1978

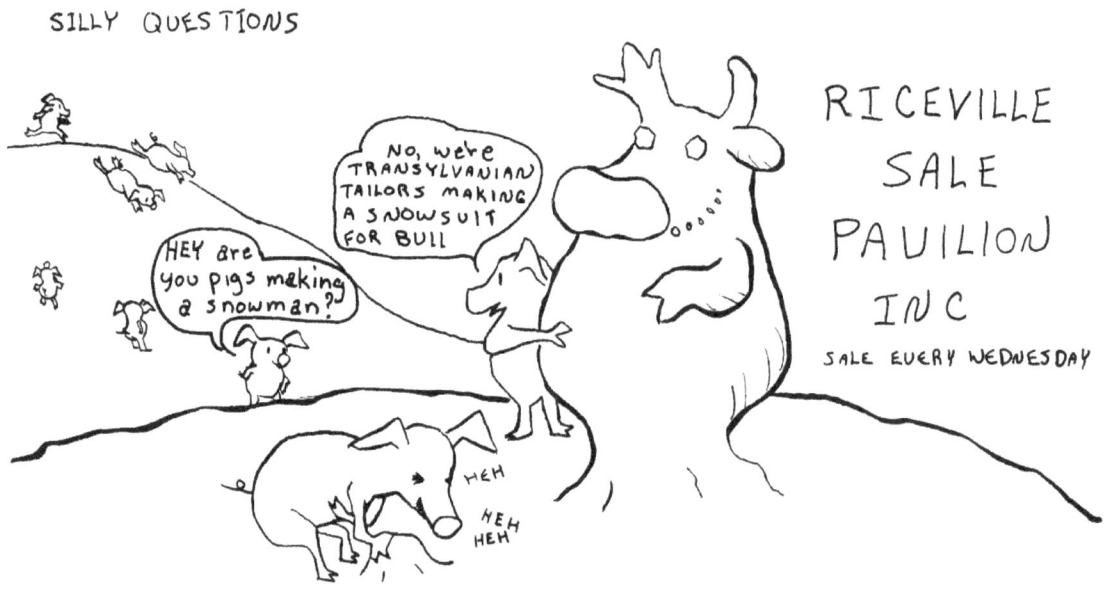

~ January 18, 1978 and February 1, 1978

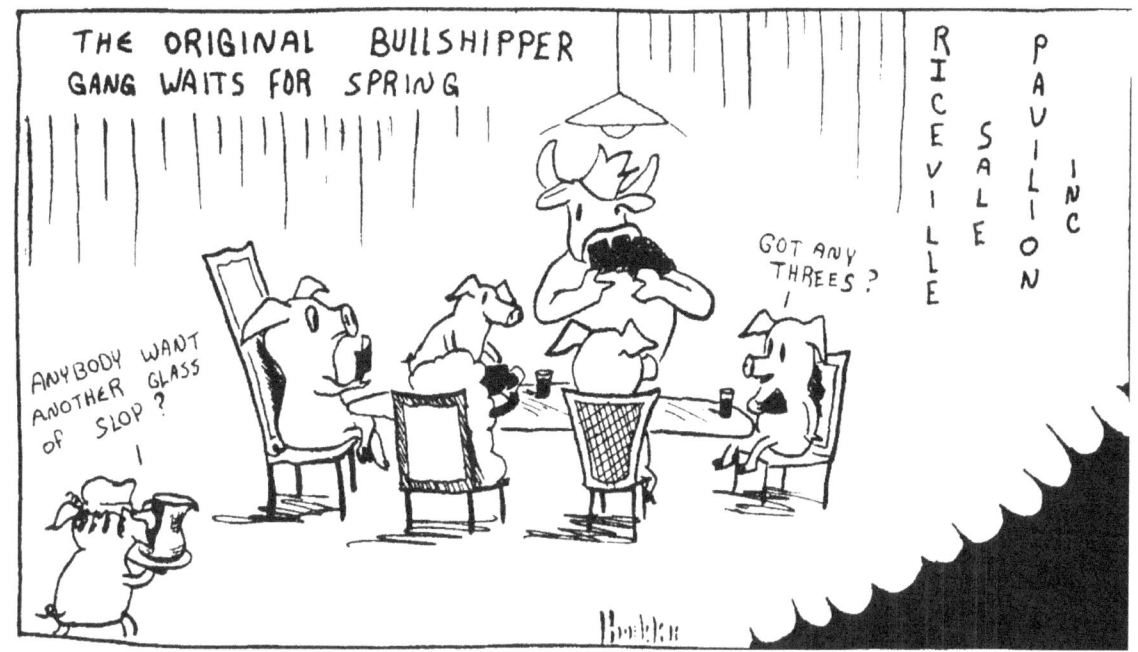

~ March 2, 1978

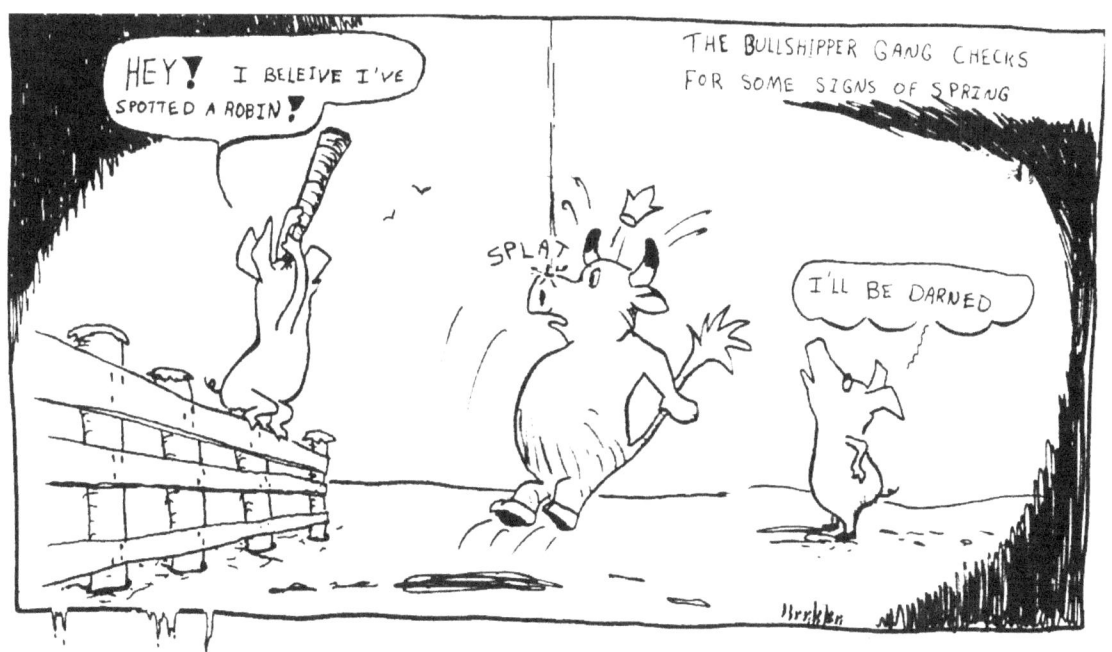

~ March 8, 1978

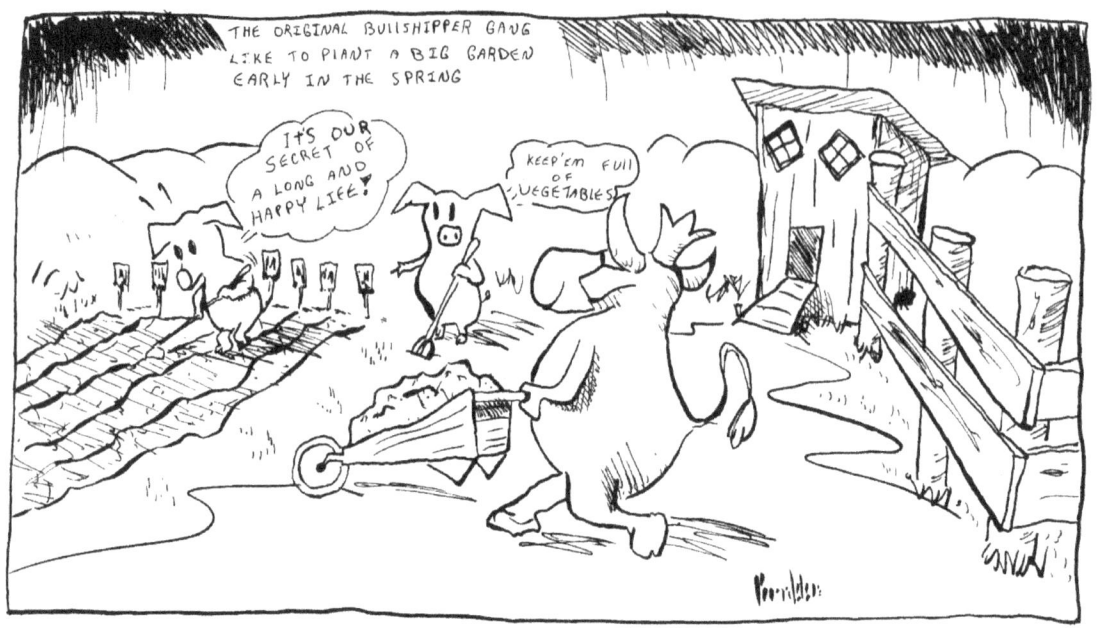

~ April 26, 1978 and May 10, 17, 24, 31, 1978

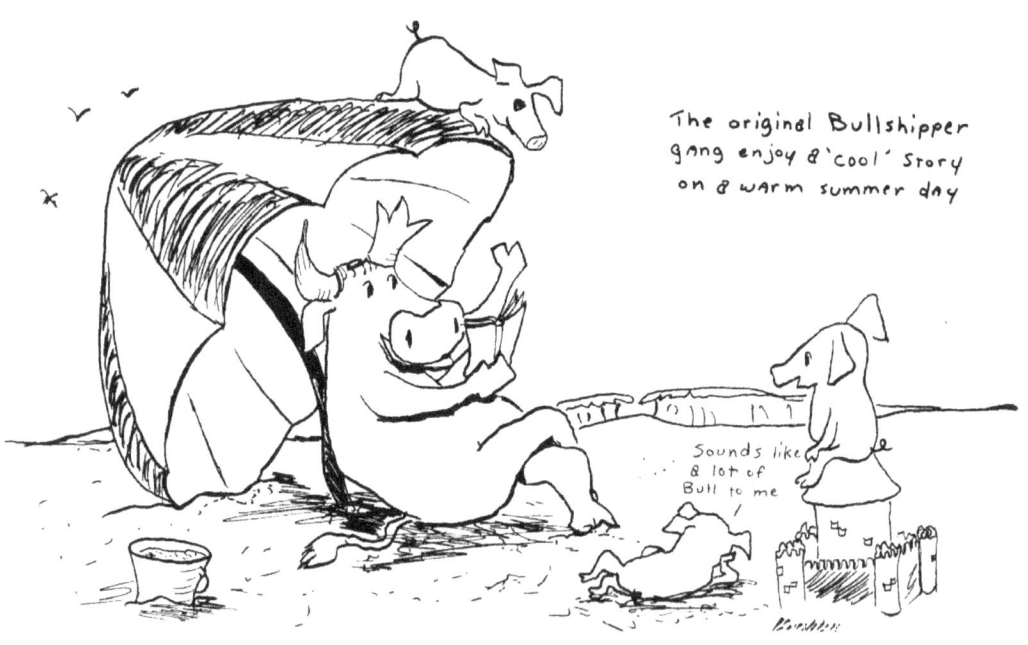

~ June 7, 14, 28, 1978

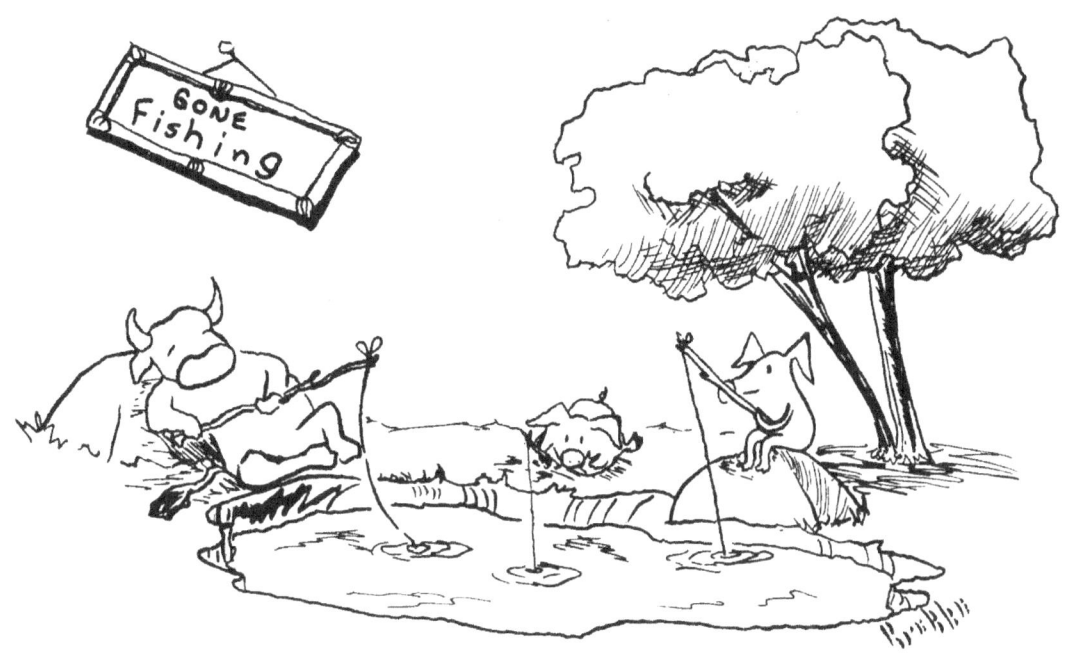

~ July 5, 12, 19, 26 1978

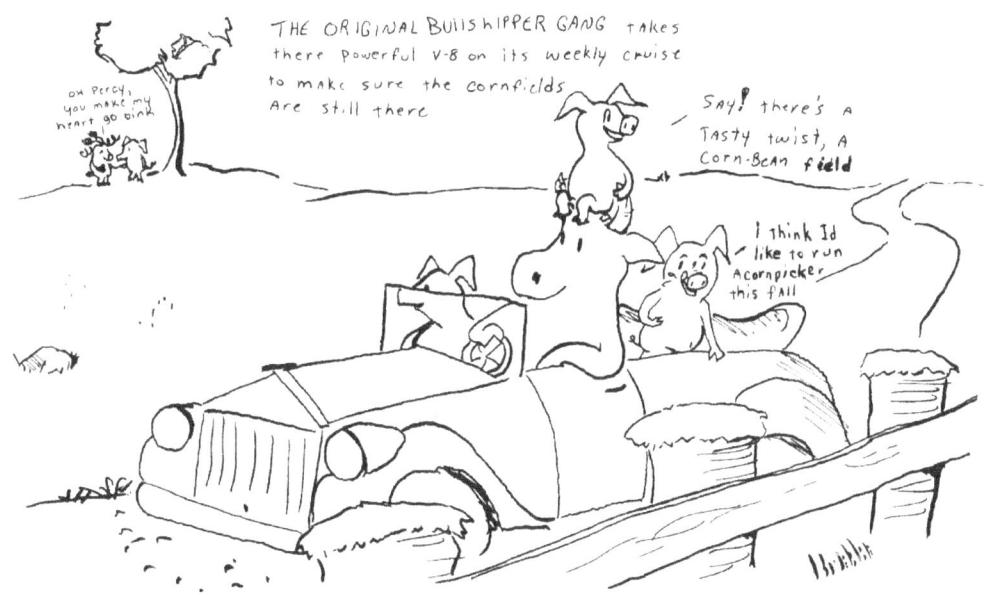

~ August 9, 23, 30 and September 6, 1978

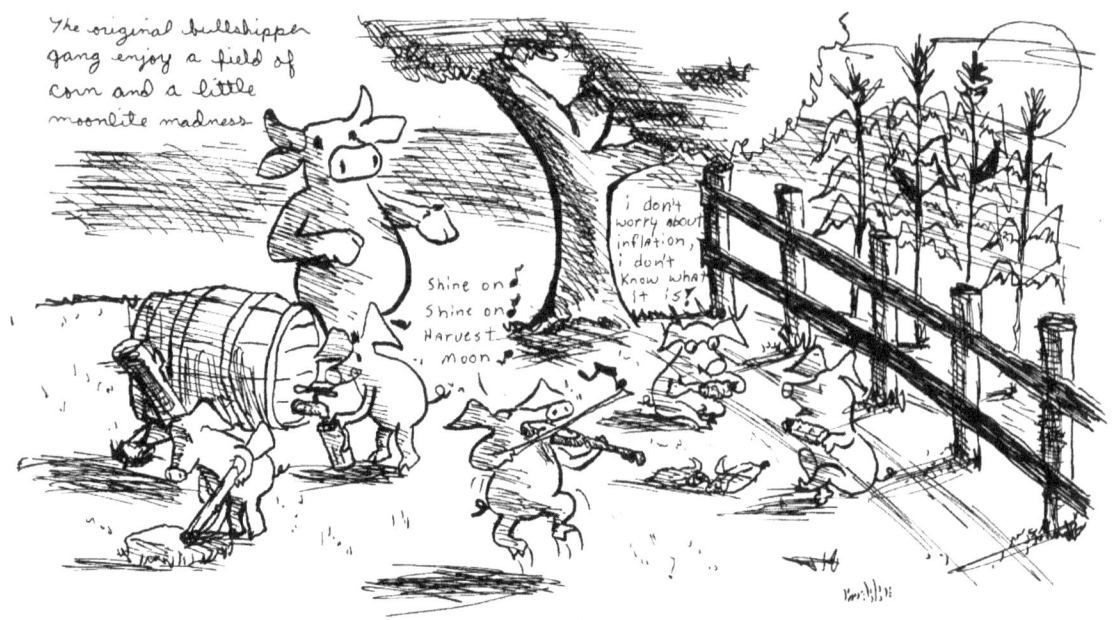

~ 1 September 13 and October 4, 11, 20, 1978

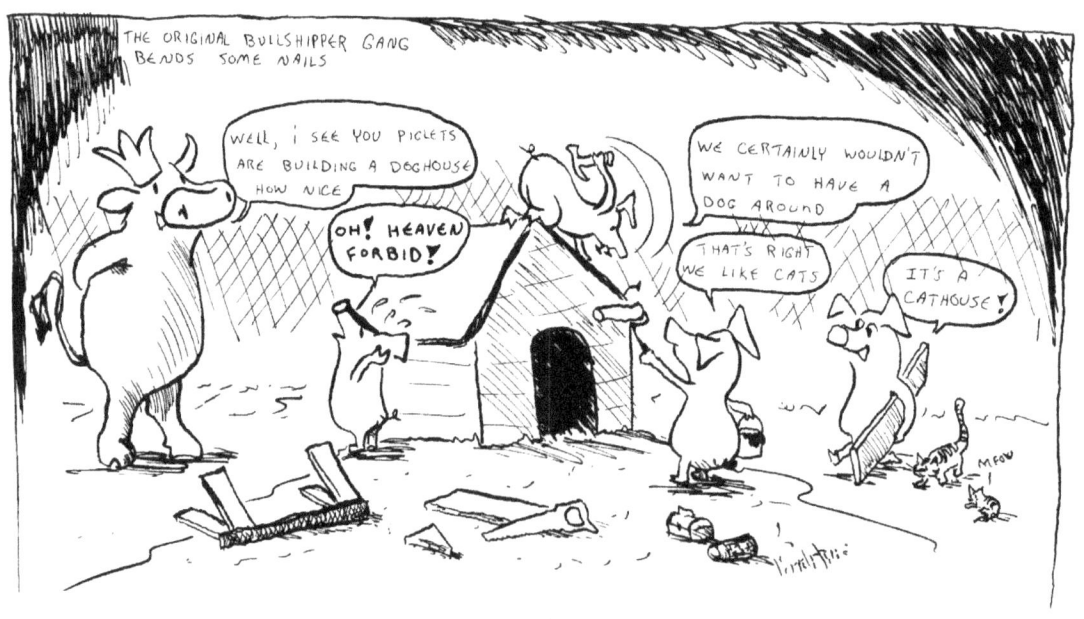

~ October 20, 25 and November 8, 15 1978

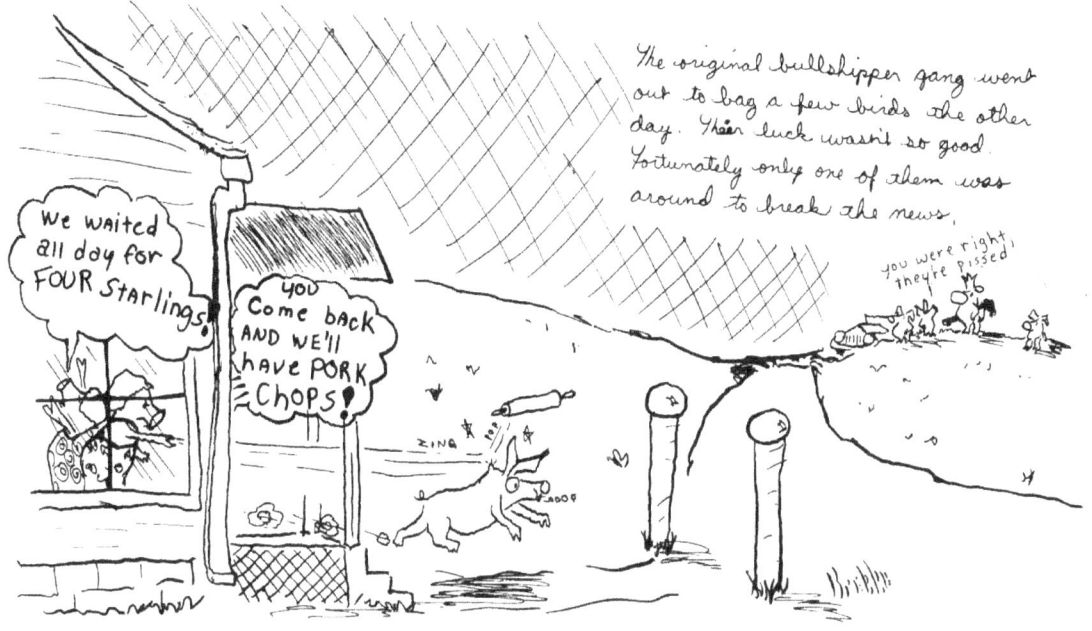

~ November 22 and December 6, 13 1978

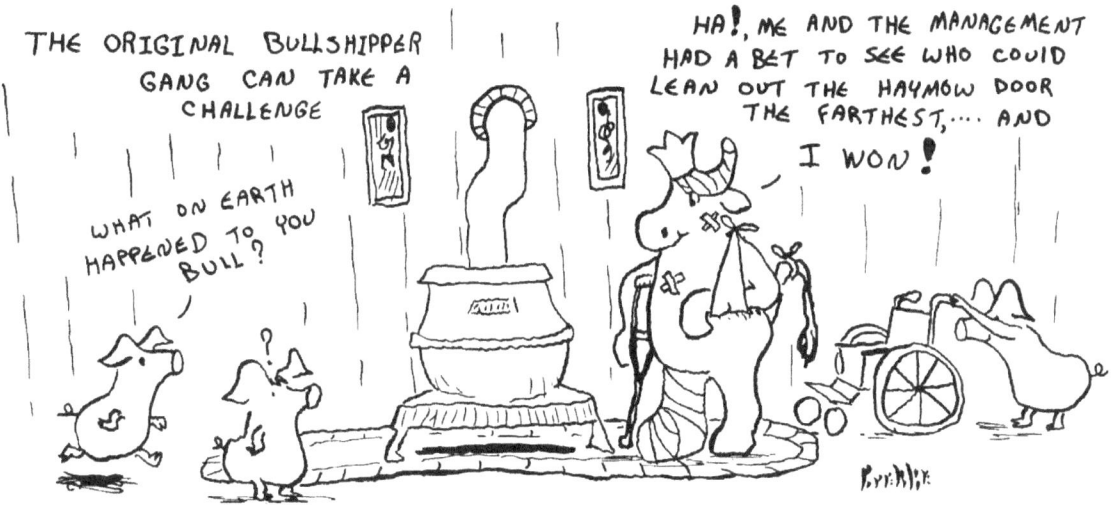

~ December 27, 1978

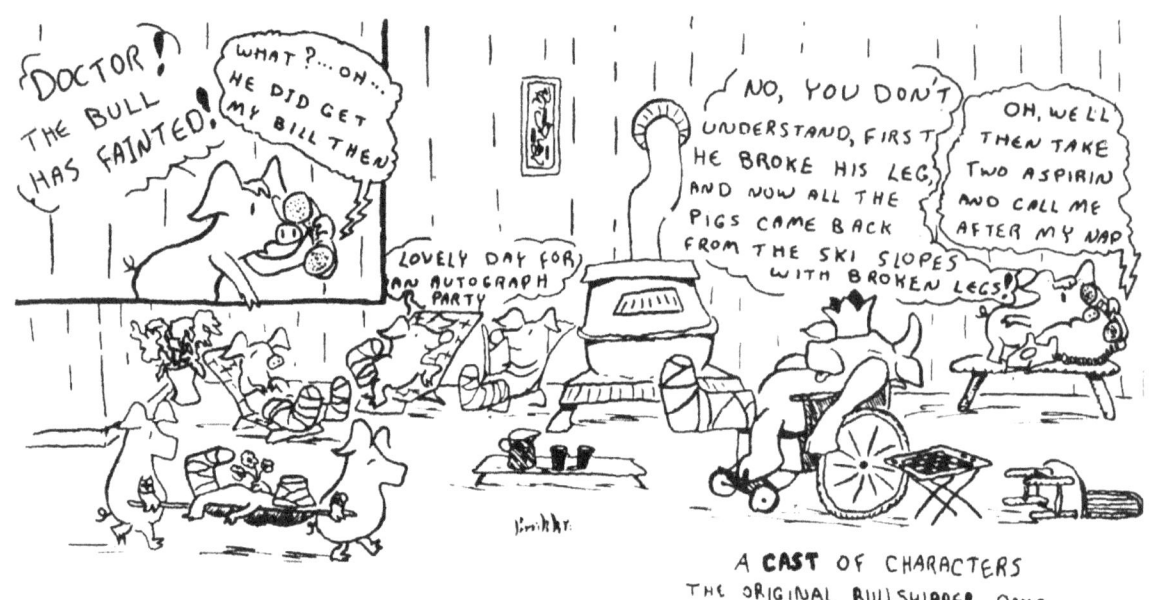

~ January 3, 1979

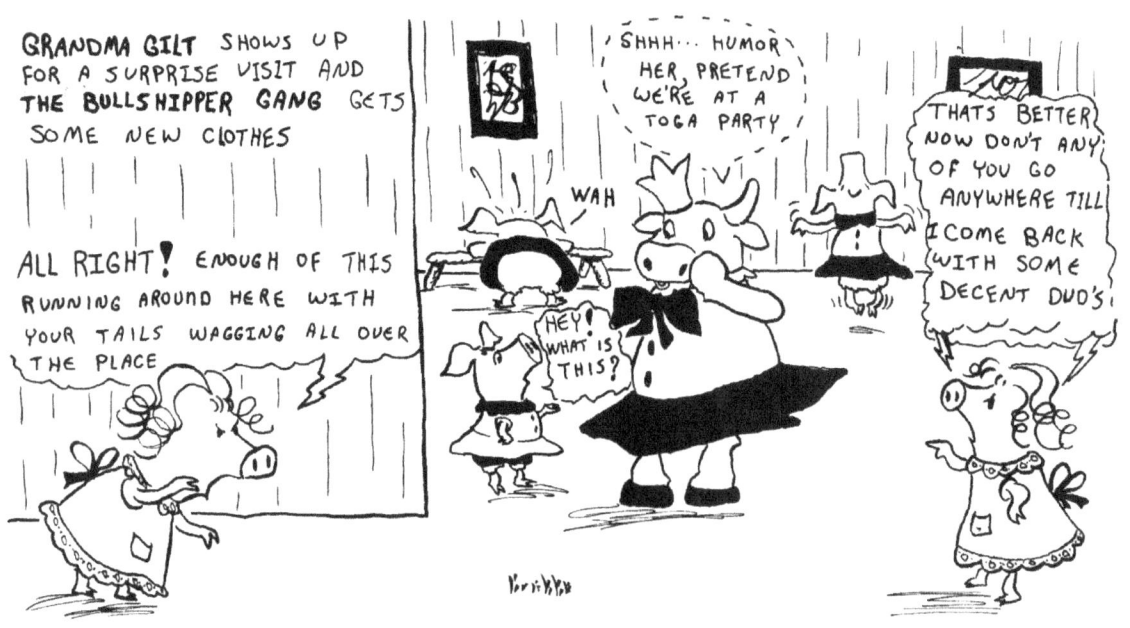

~ January 10, 1979

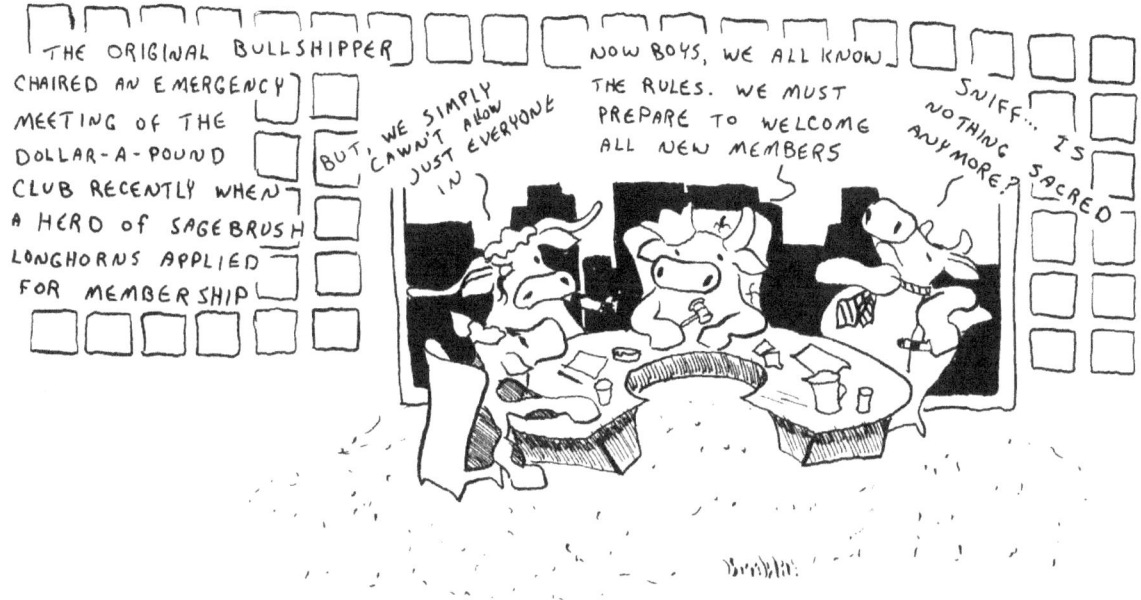

~ January 7, 1979

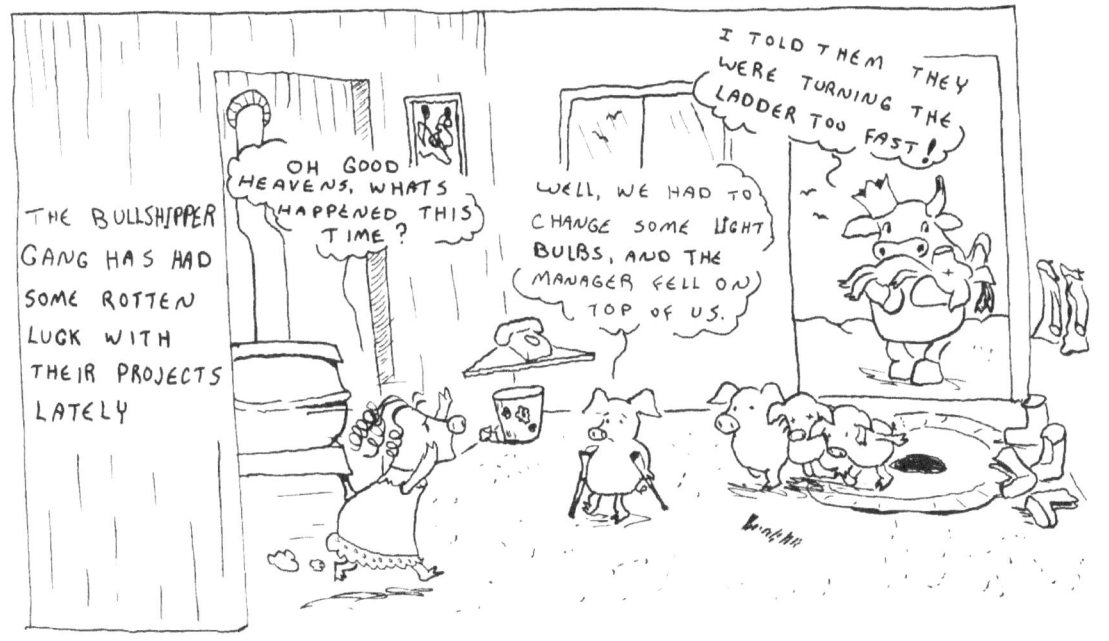

~ January 24, 1979

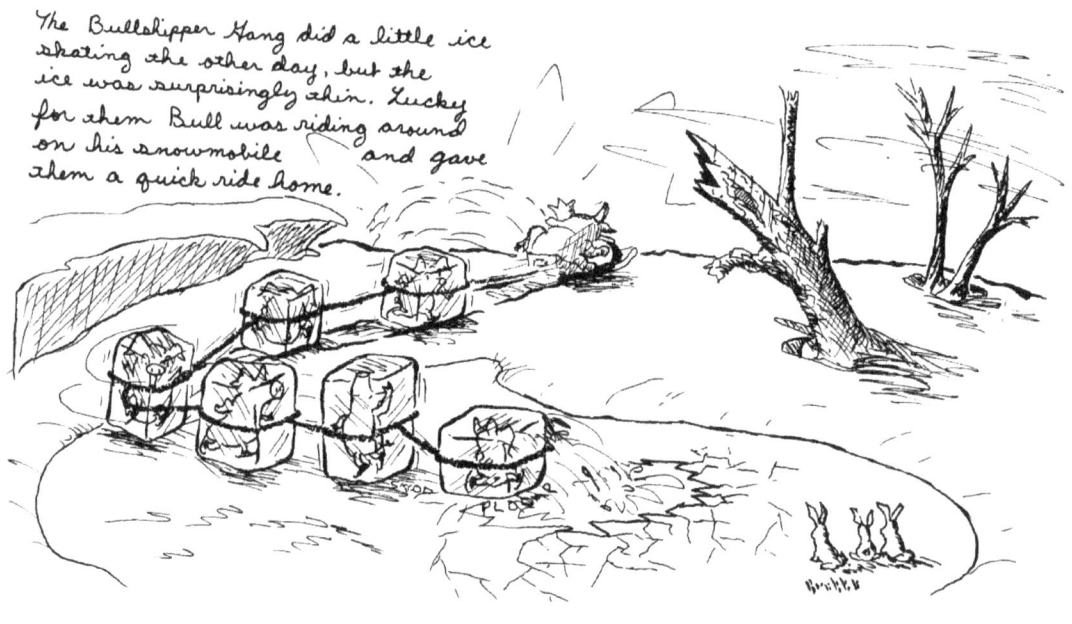

~ January 31, 1979

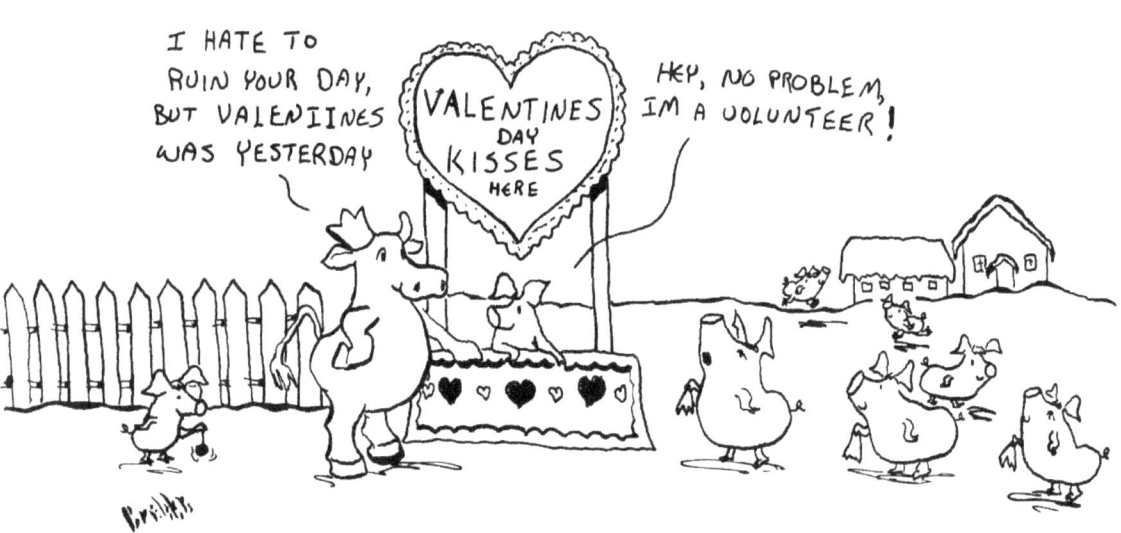

~ February 7, 1979

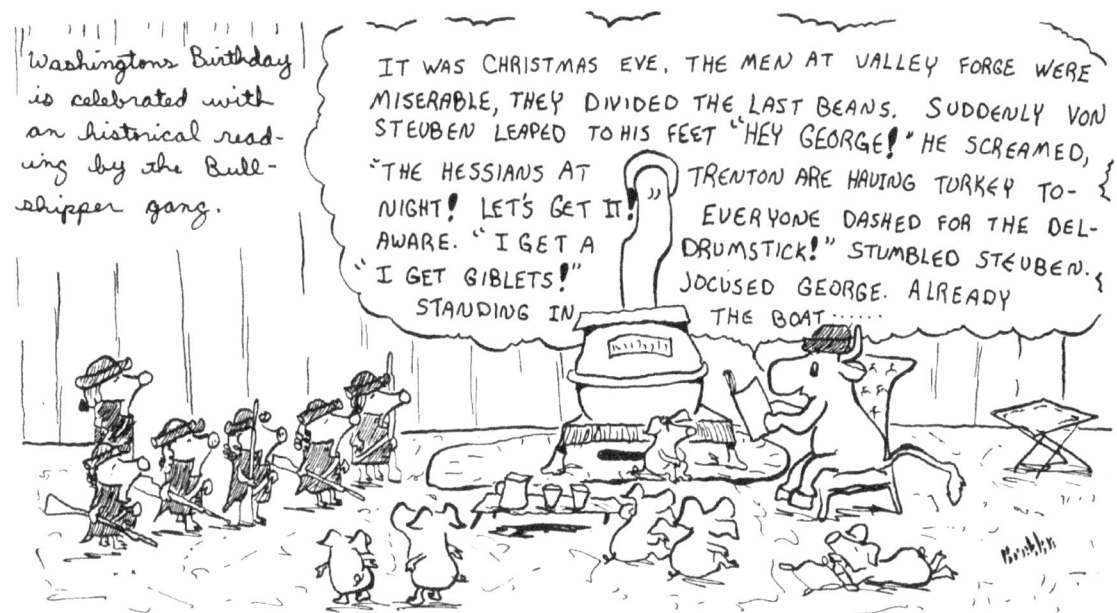

~ February 14, 1979

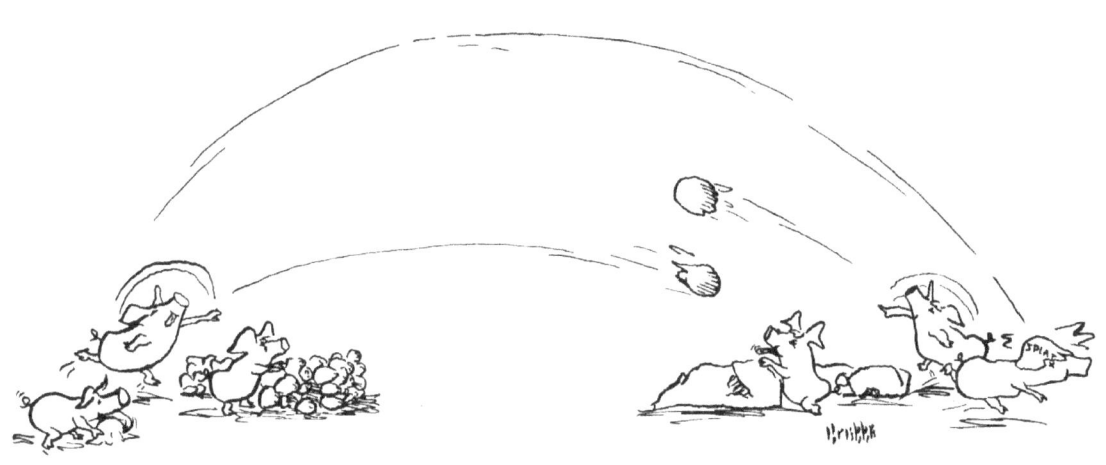

~ February 21, 1979

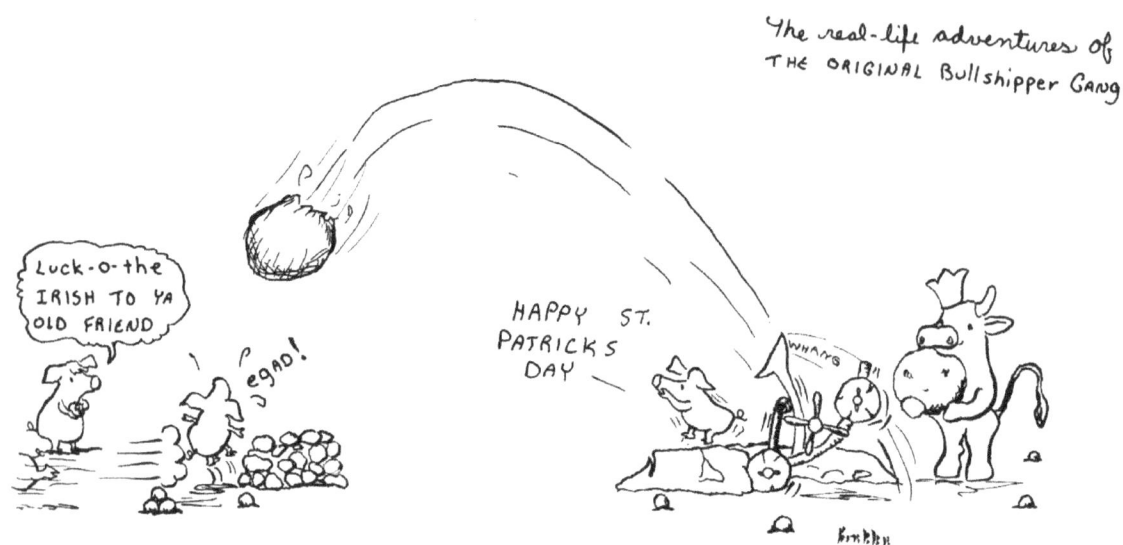

Part II of Le SNOWBALL FIGHT

~ February 28, 1979

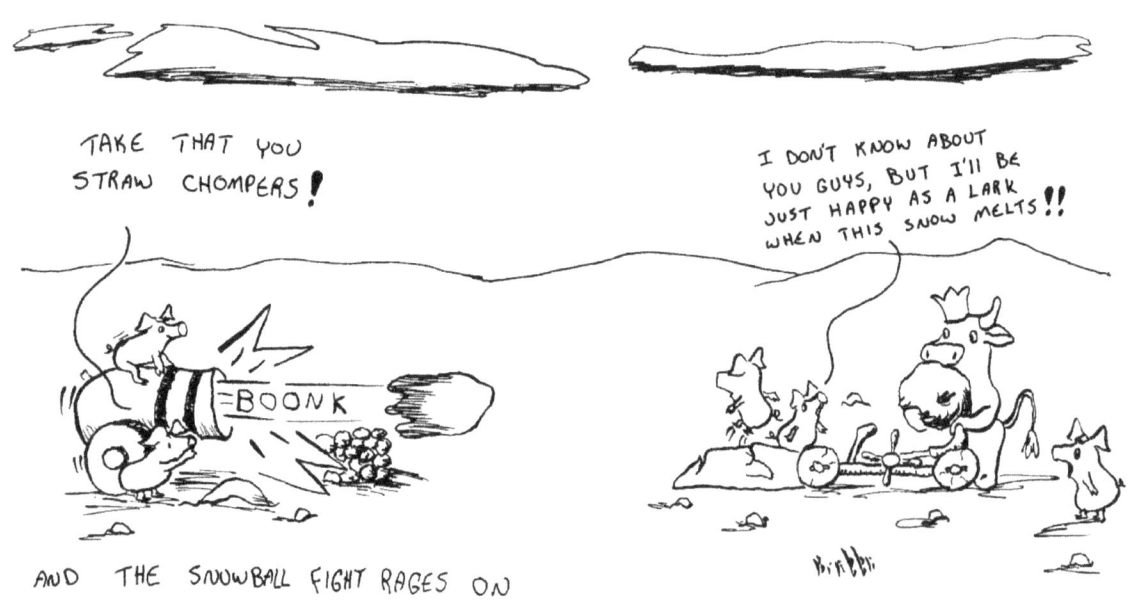

AND THE SNOWBALL FIGHT RAGES ON

~ March 7, 1979

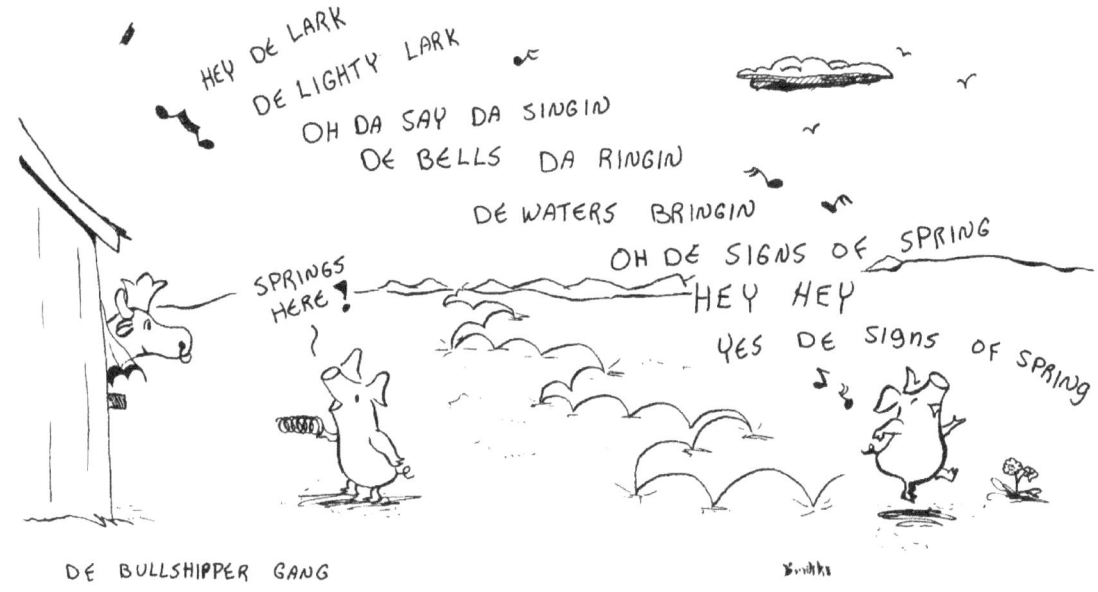

~ March 14, 1979

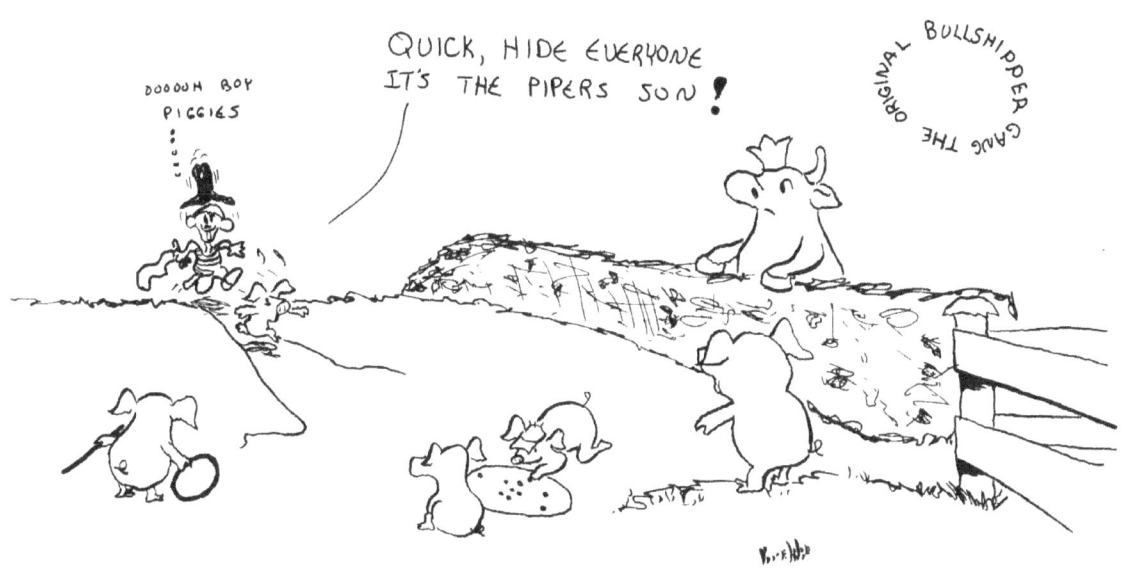

~ March 21, 1979

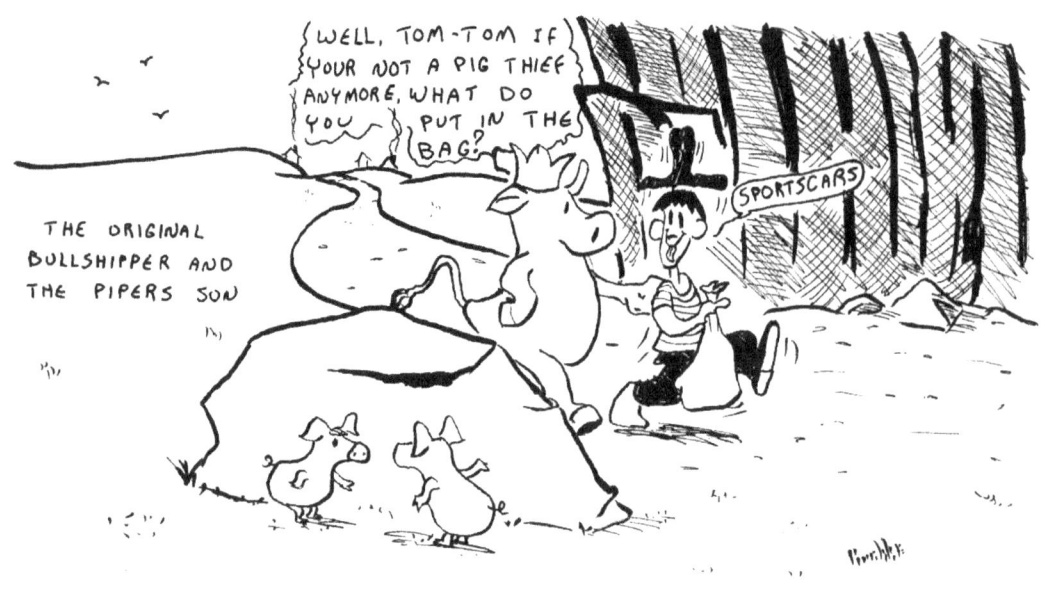

~ March 28, 1979

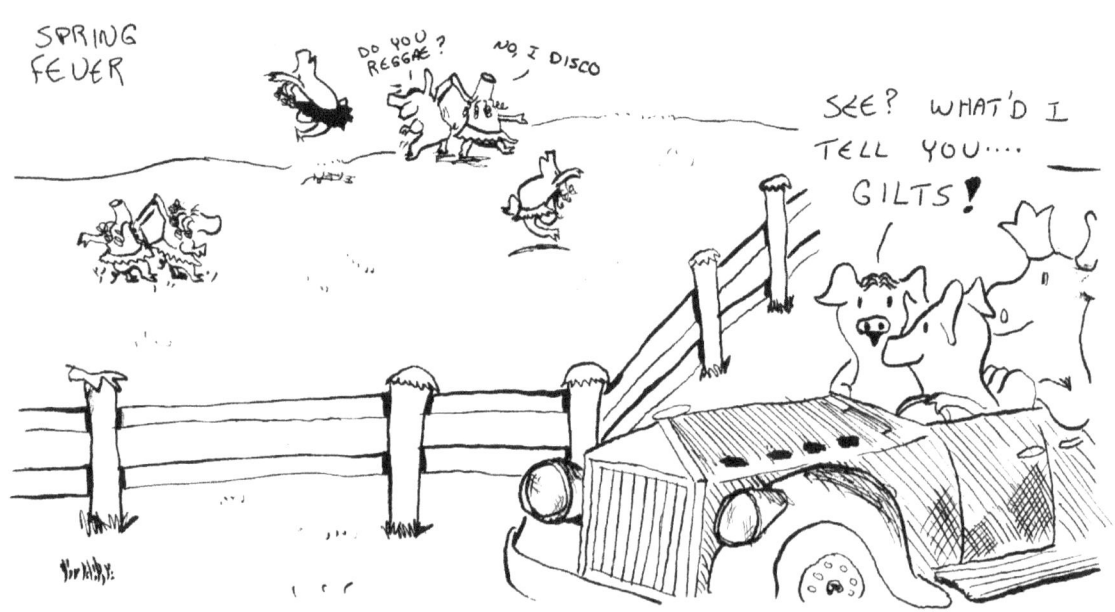

~ April 4, 1979

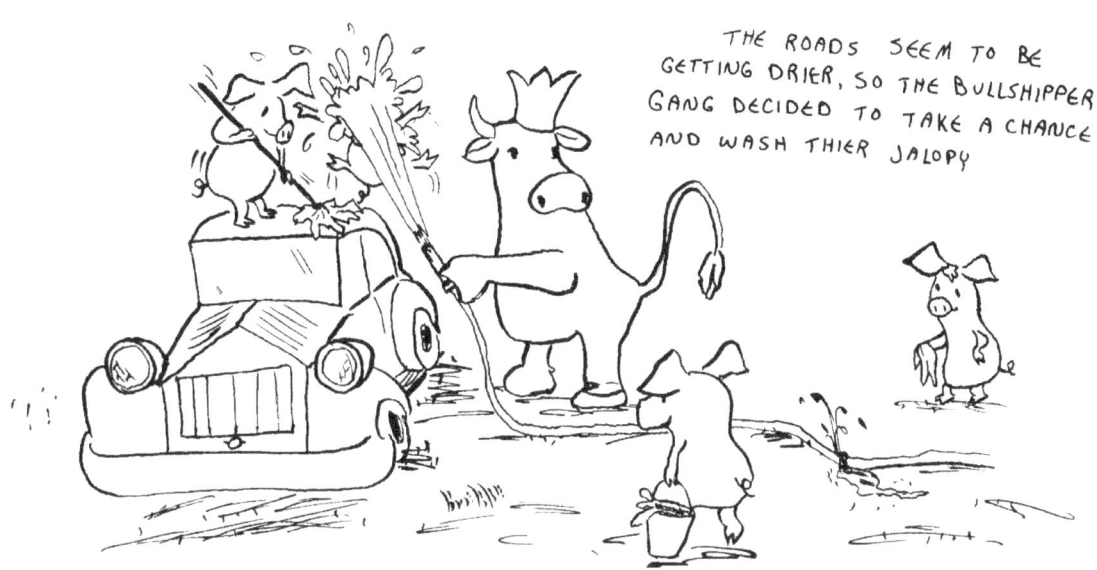

~ April 11, 1979

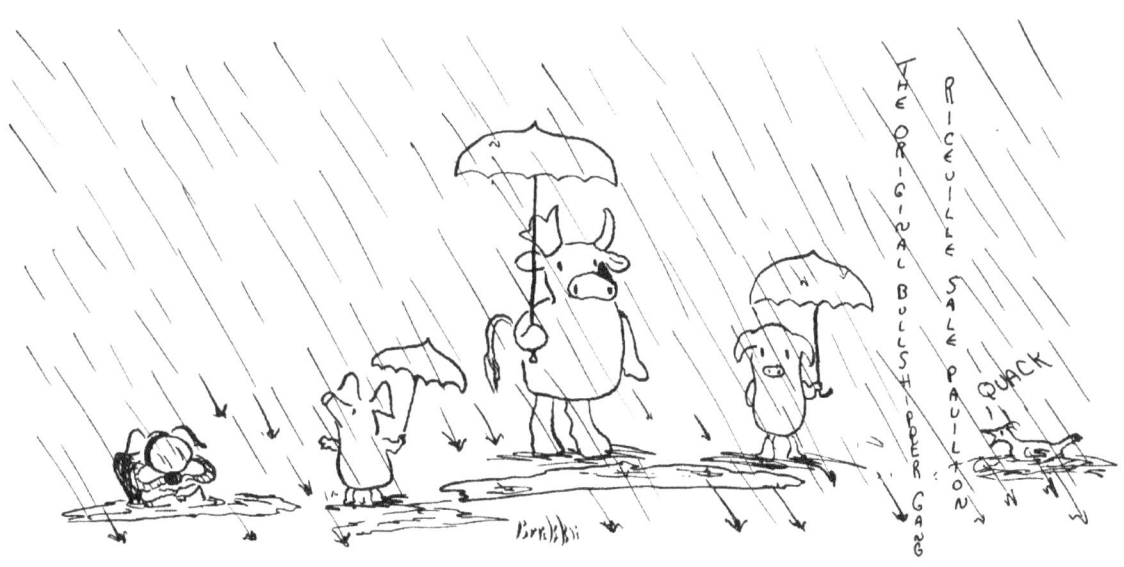

~ April 18, 1979

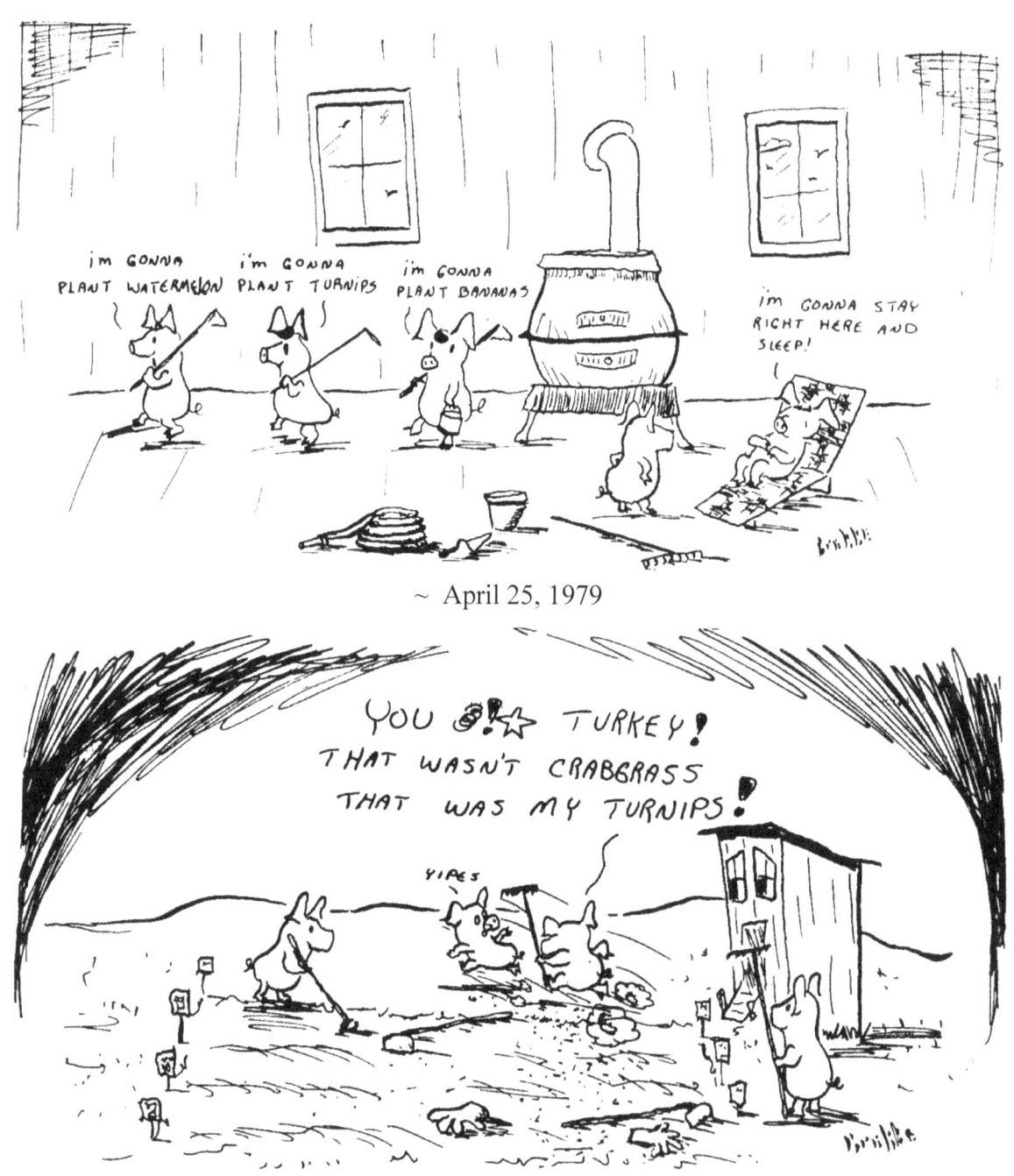

~ April 25, 1979

~ May 2, 1979

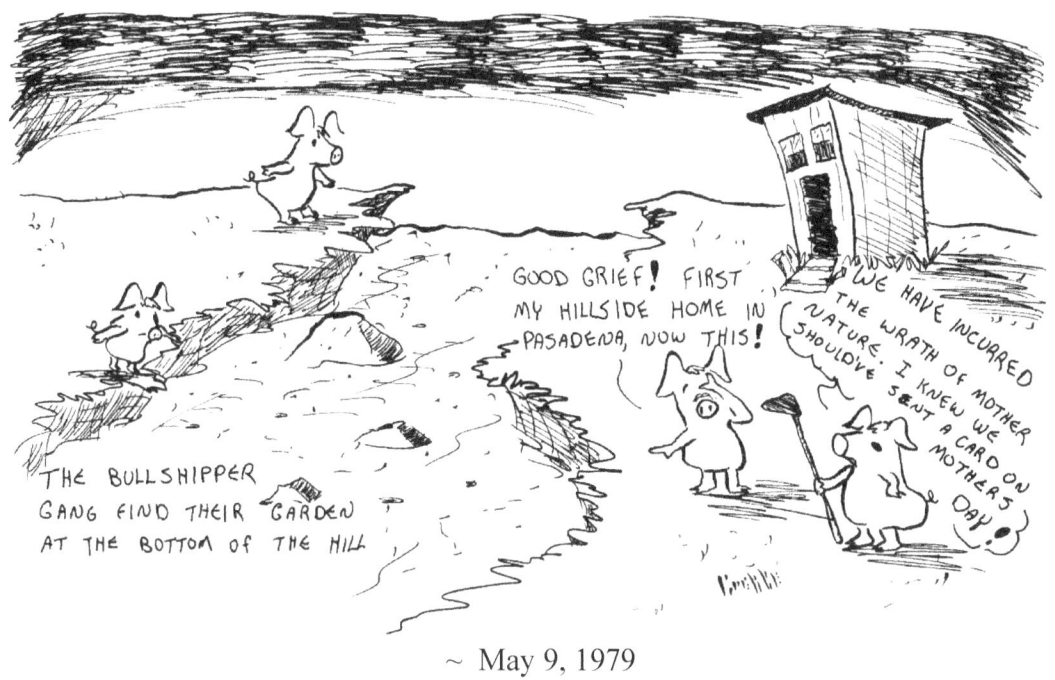

~ May 9, 1979

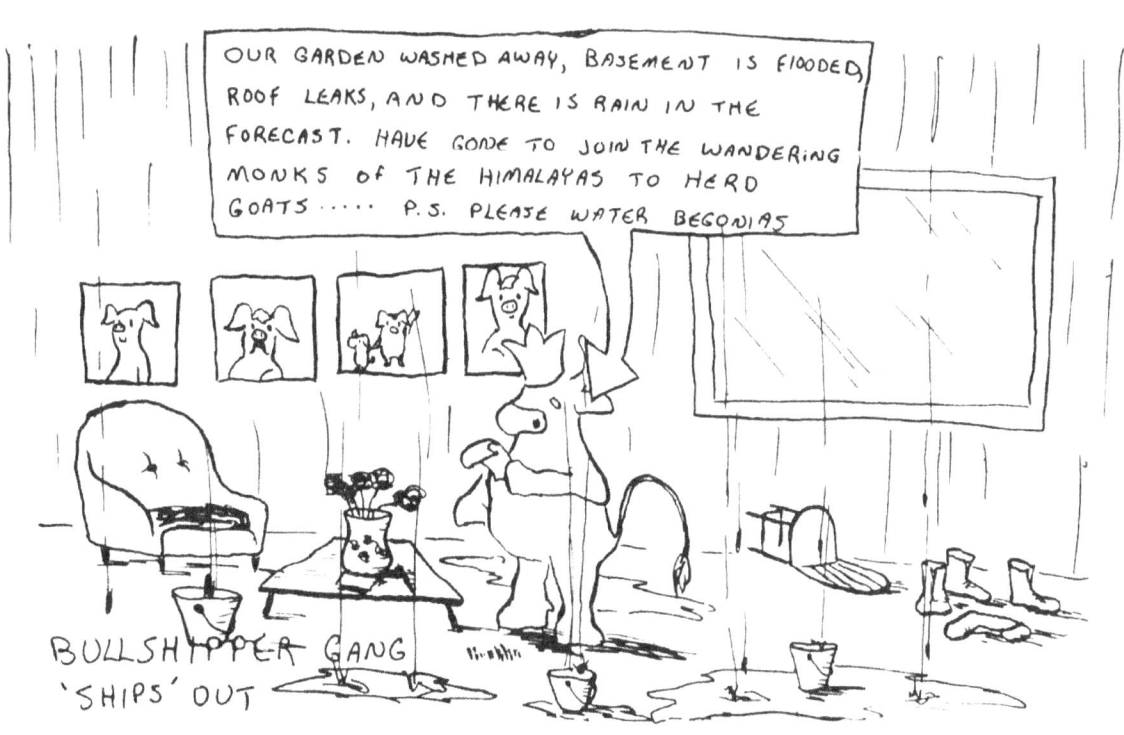

~ May 16, 1979

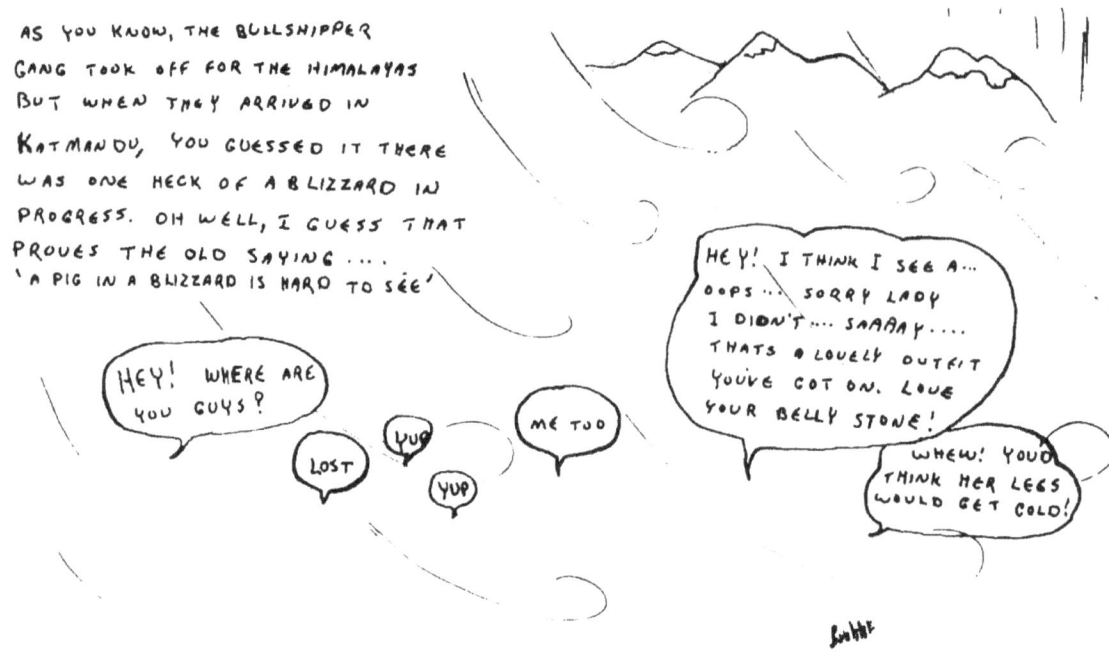

~ May 23, 1979

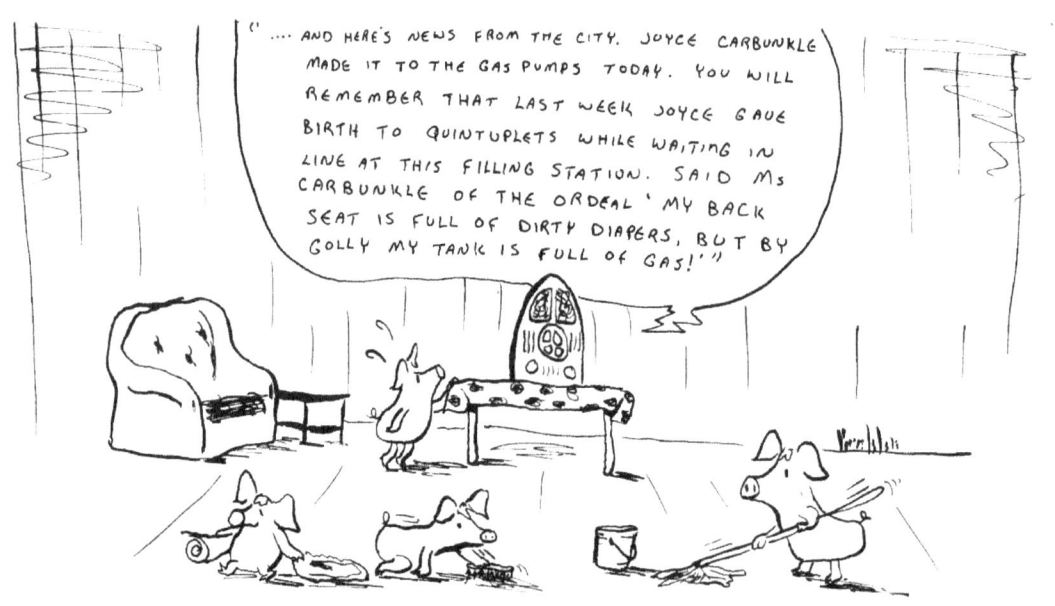

~ May 30, 1979

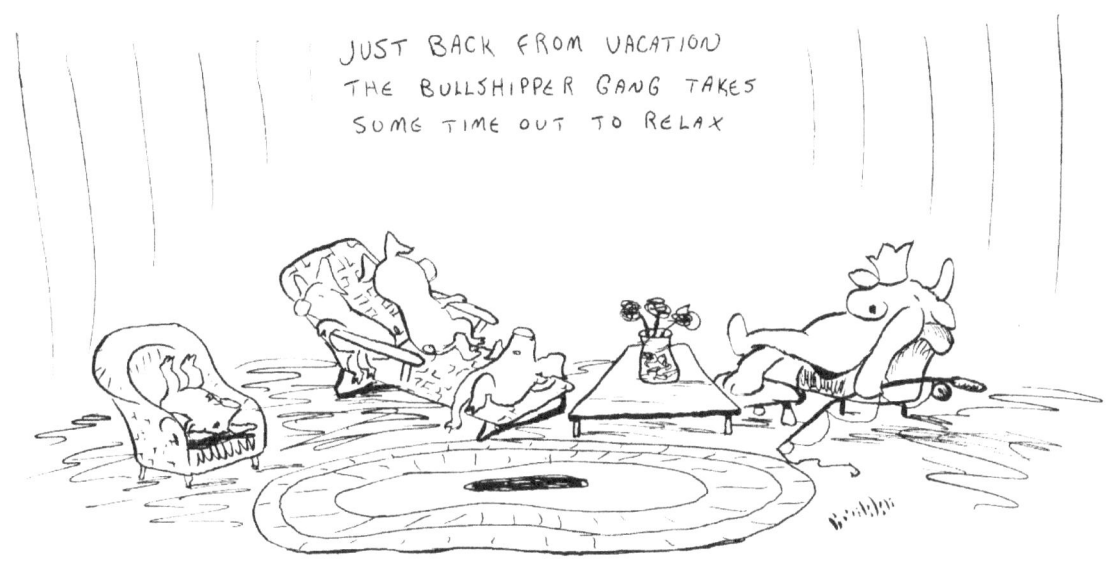

~ June 13, 1979

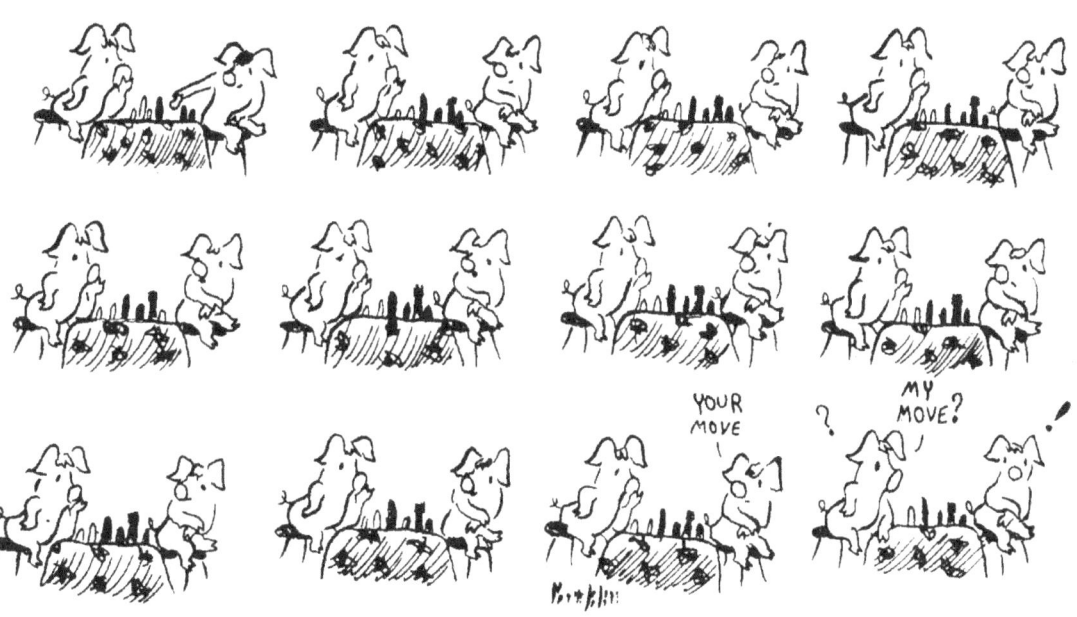

~ June 20, 1979

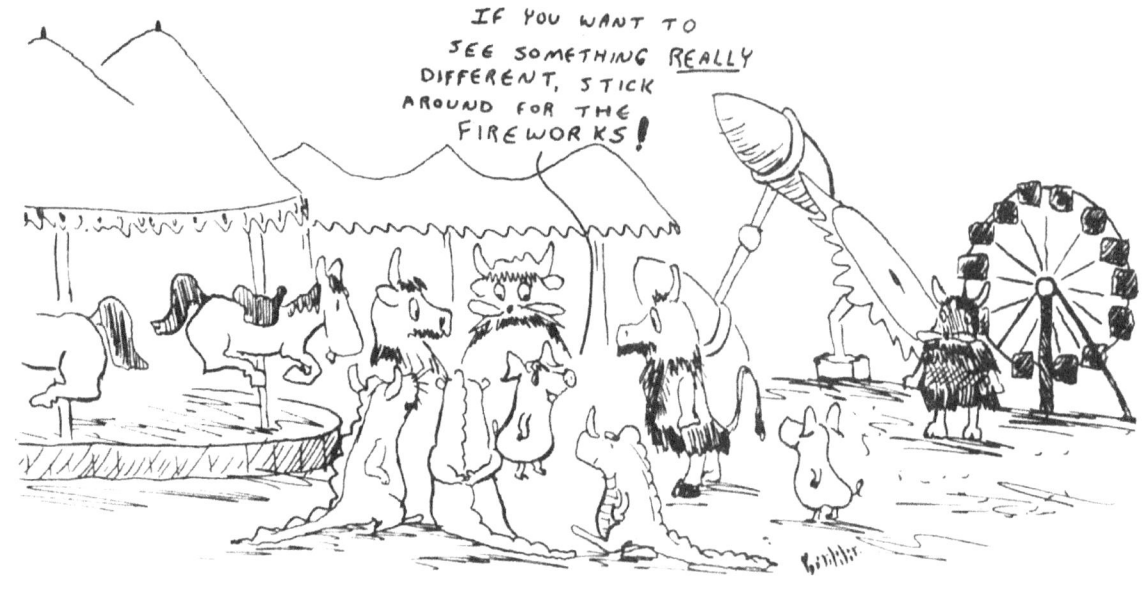

~ June 27, 1979

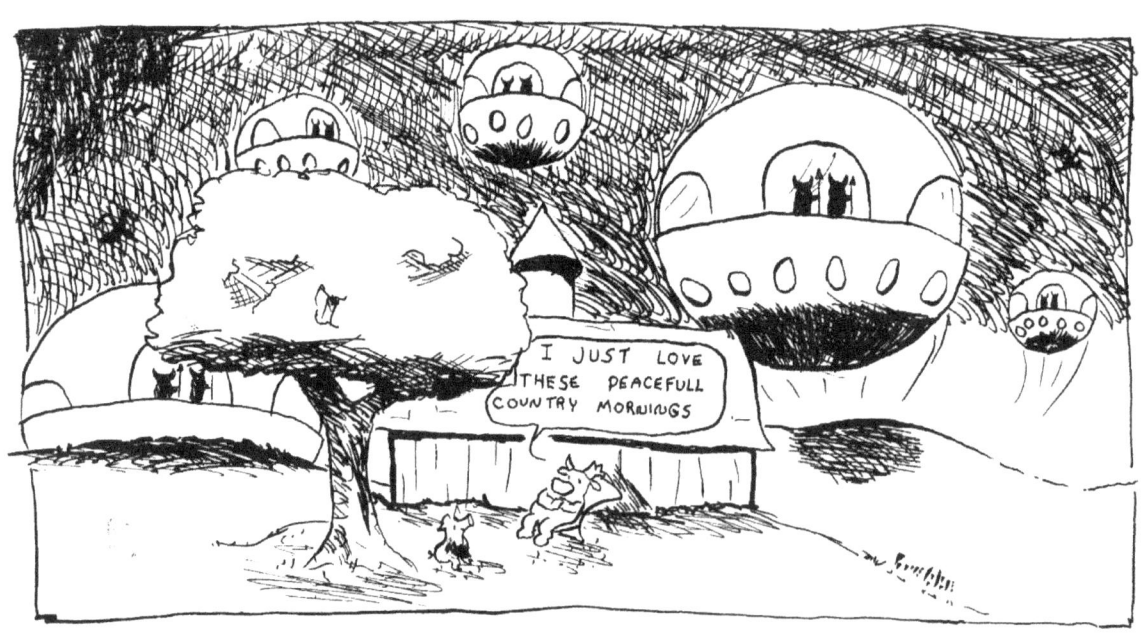

~ July 4, 1979

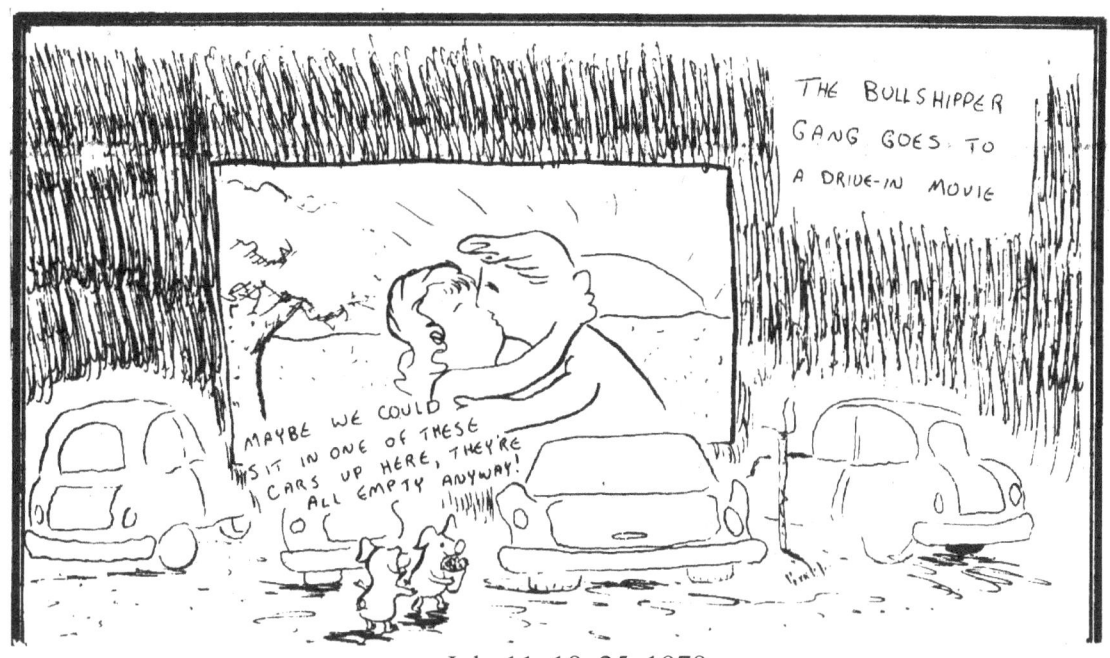

~ July 11, 18, 25, 1979

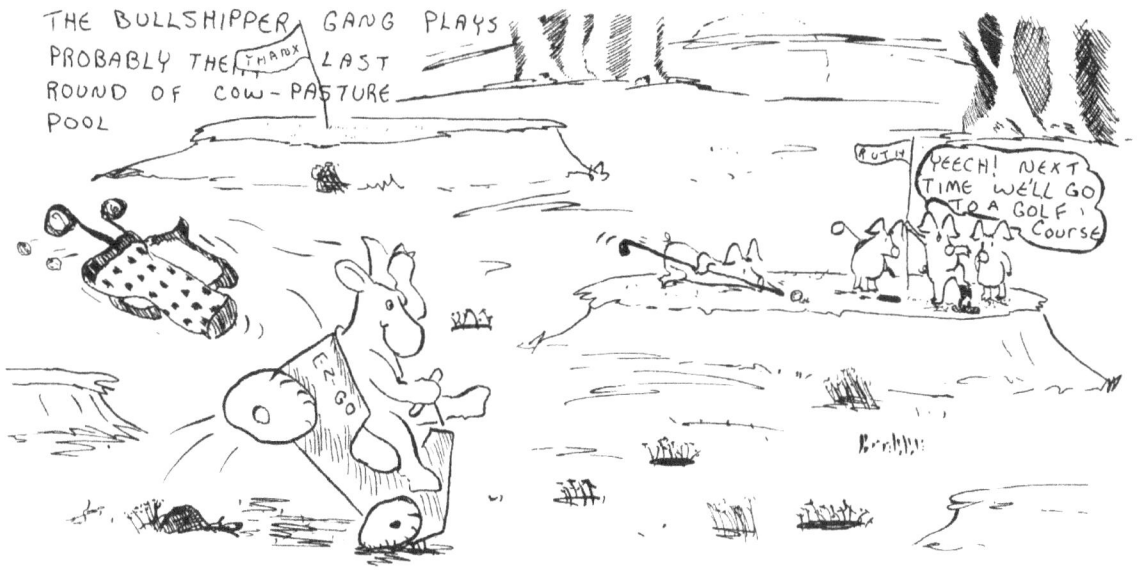

~ August 1, 1979

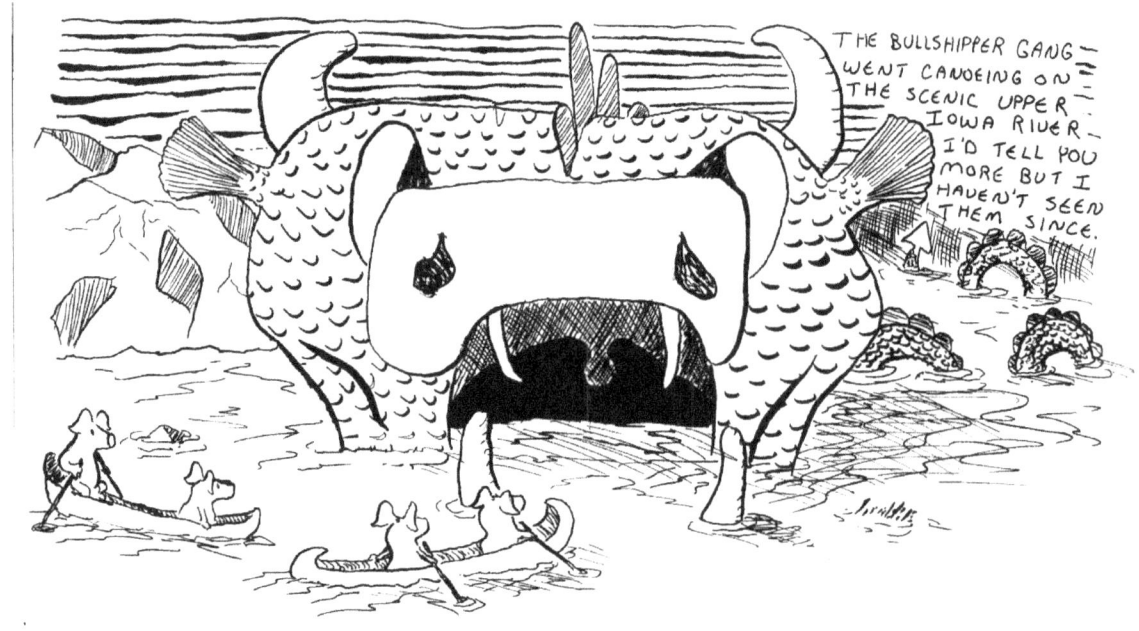

~ August 8, 1979

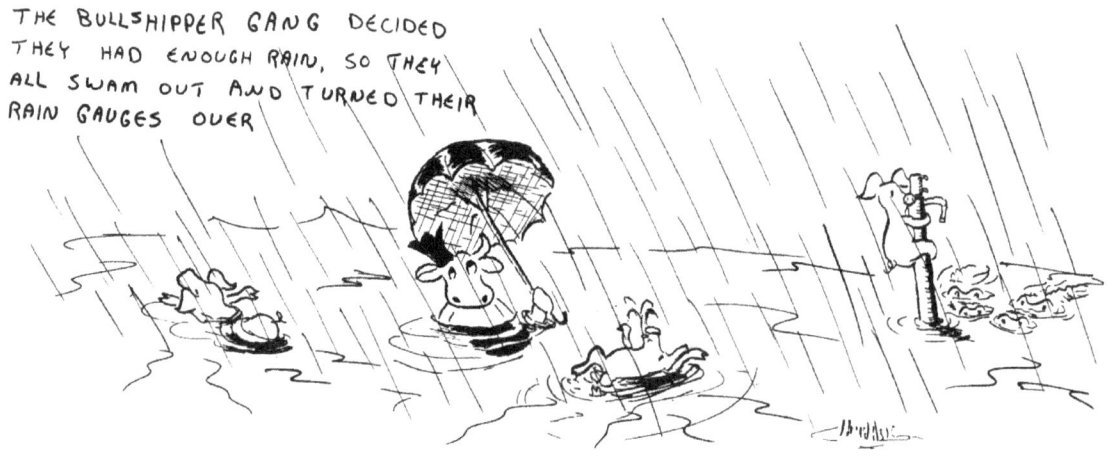

~ August 15, 1979

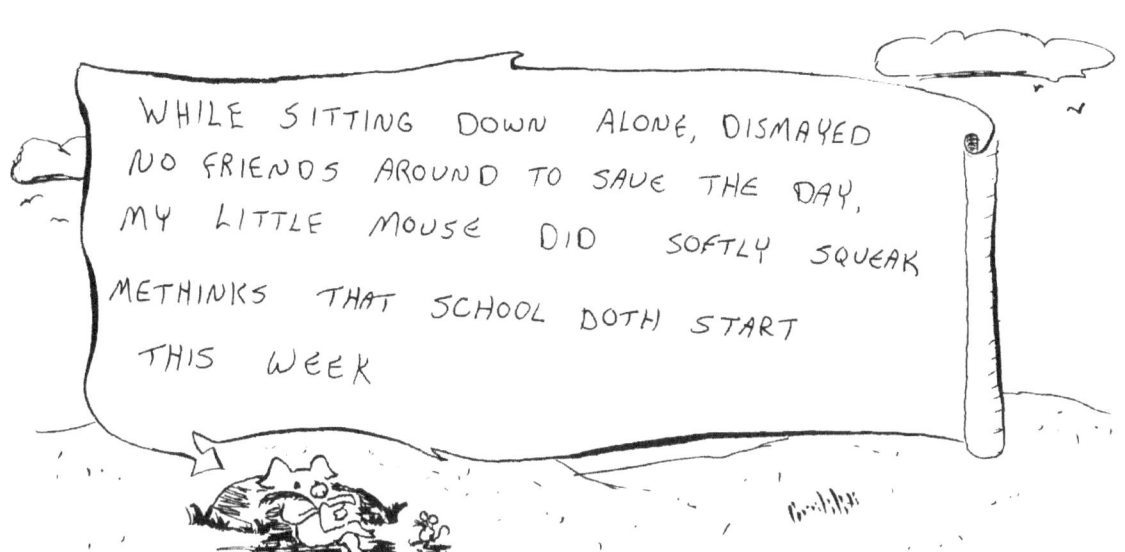

~ August 22, 1979

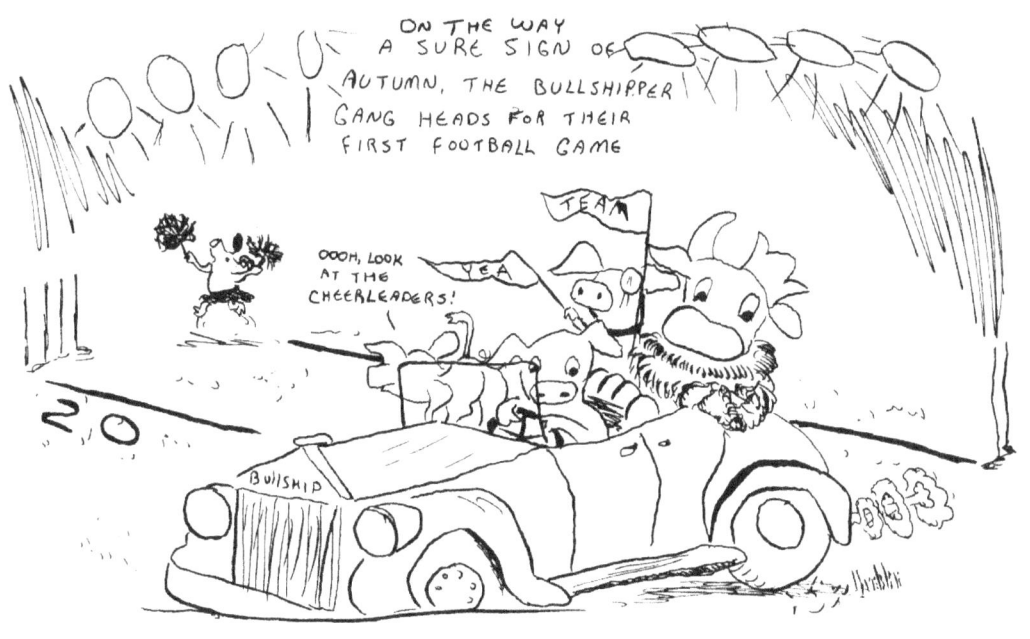

~ August 29, 1979

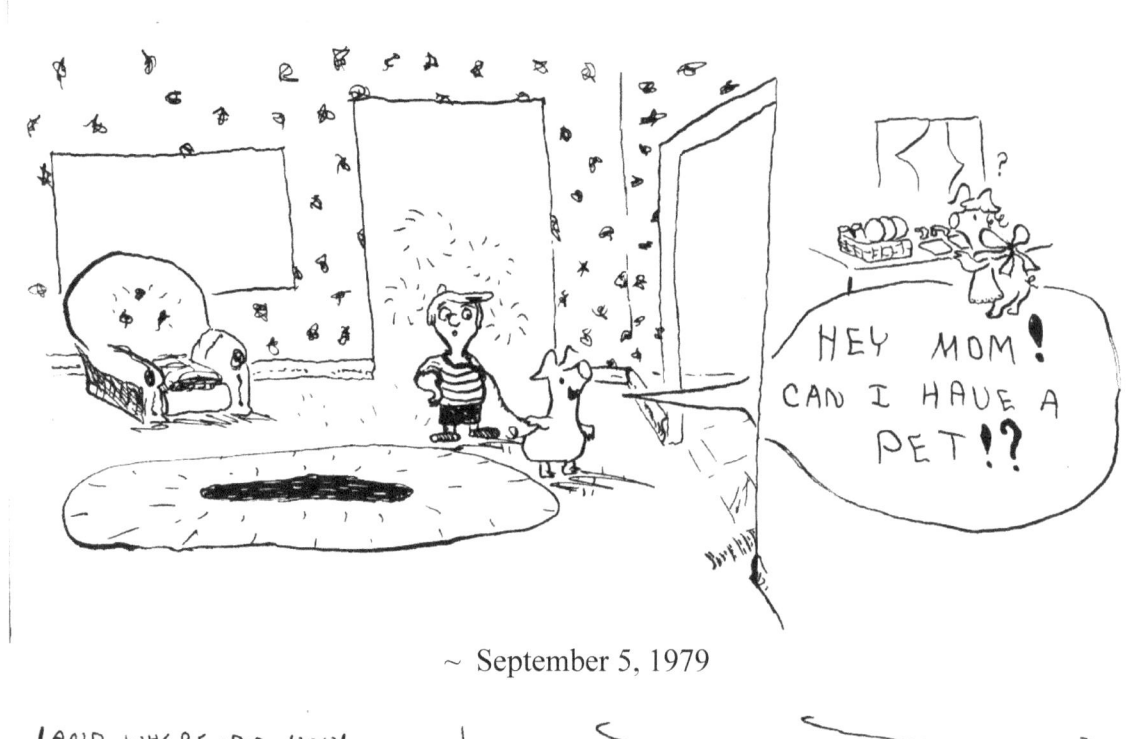

~ September 5, 1979

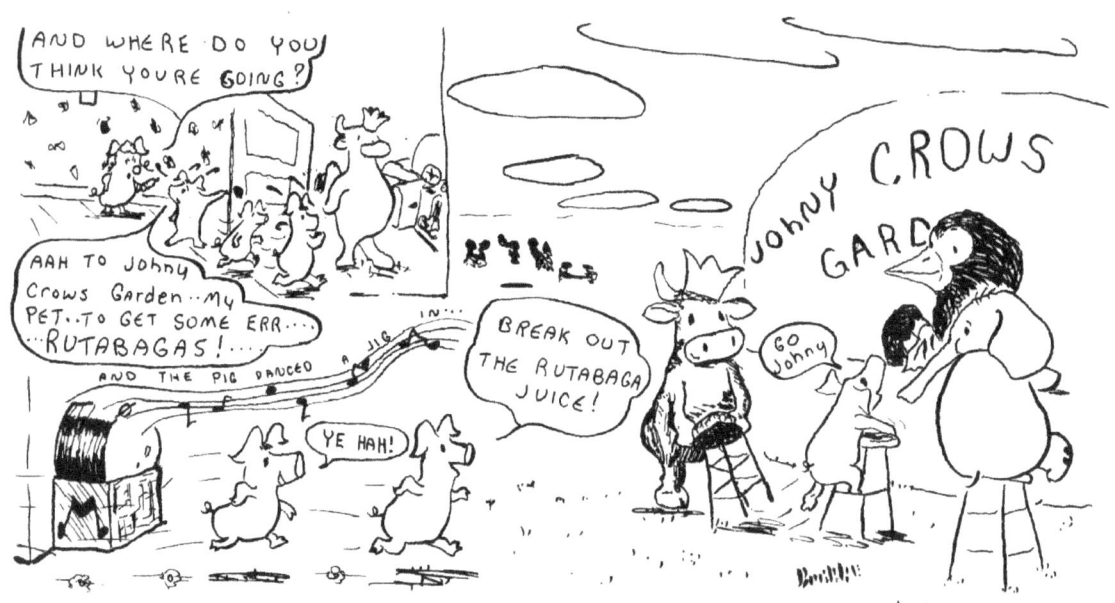

~ September 12, 1979

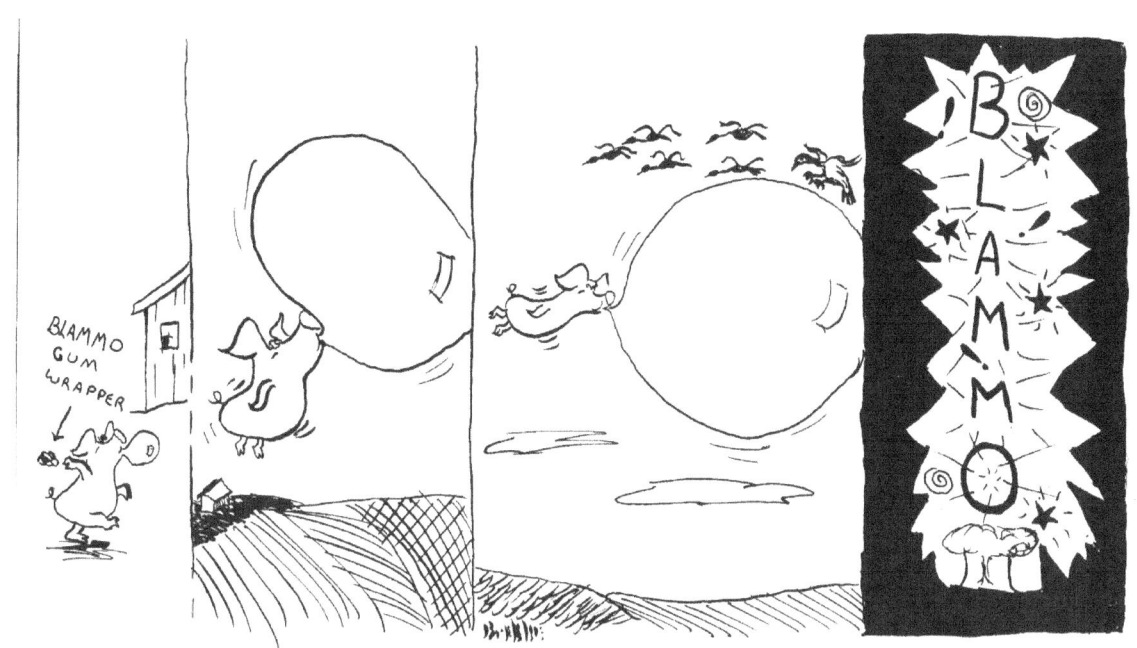

~ September 19, 1979

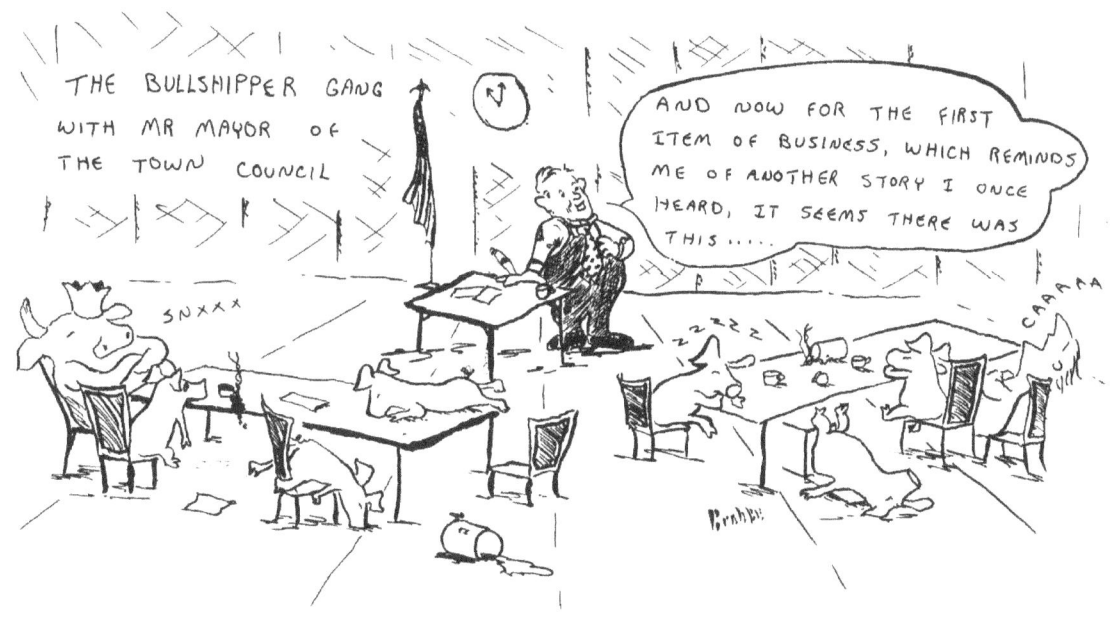

~ September 26, 1979

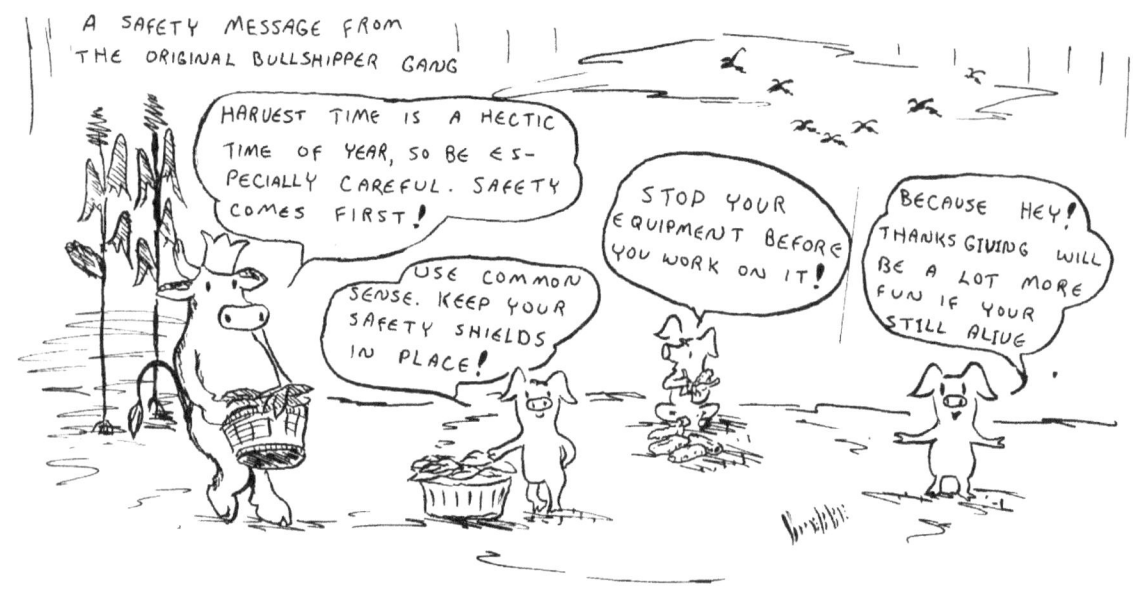

~ October 3, 1979

~ October 10, 1979

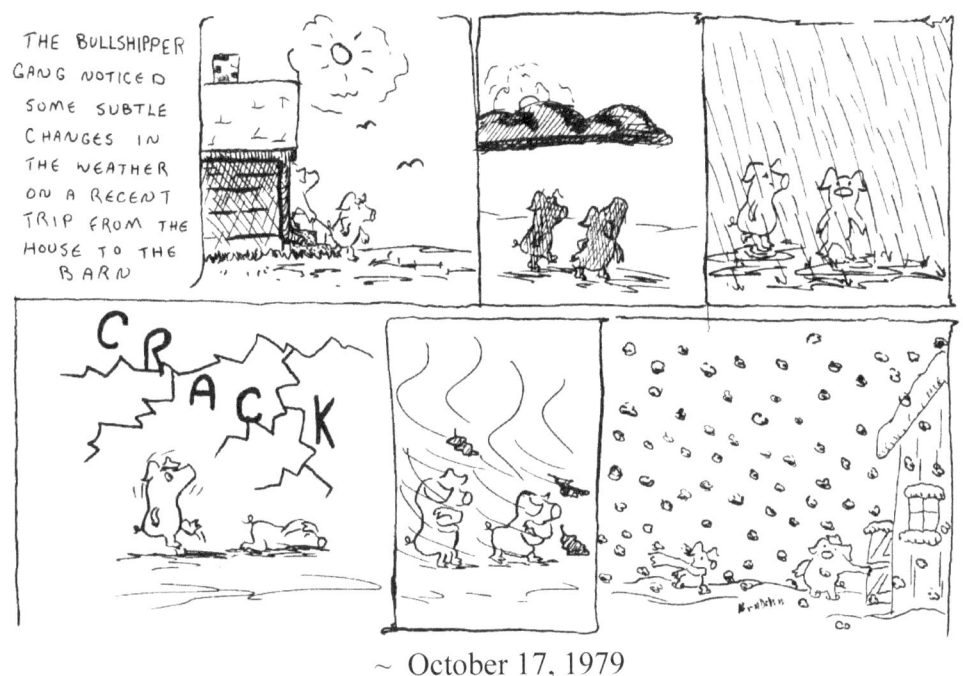

~ October 17, 1979

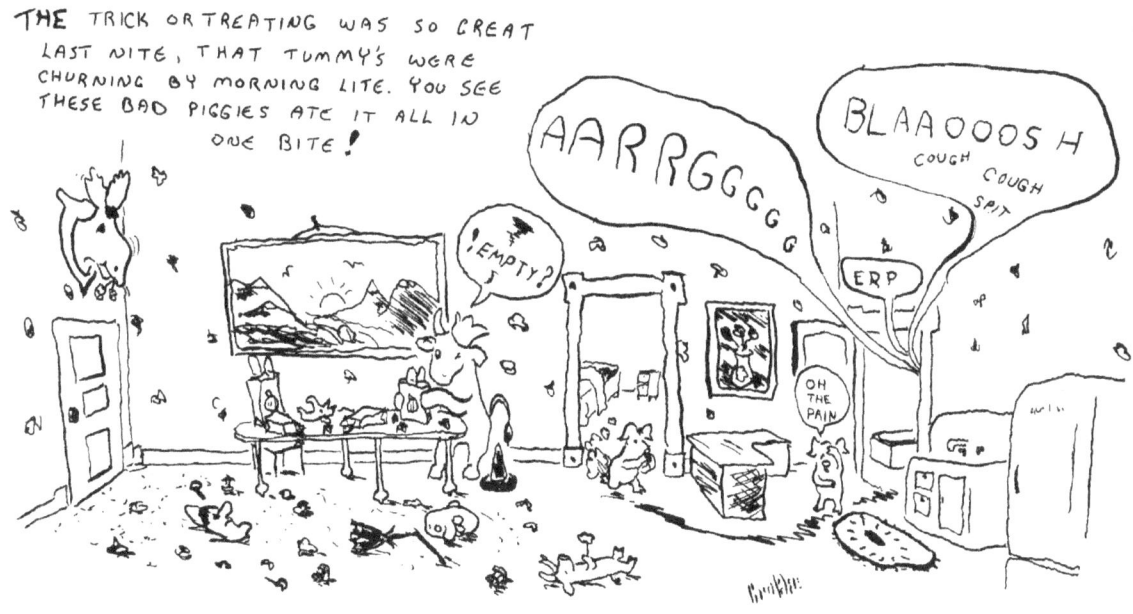

~ October 24, 1979

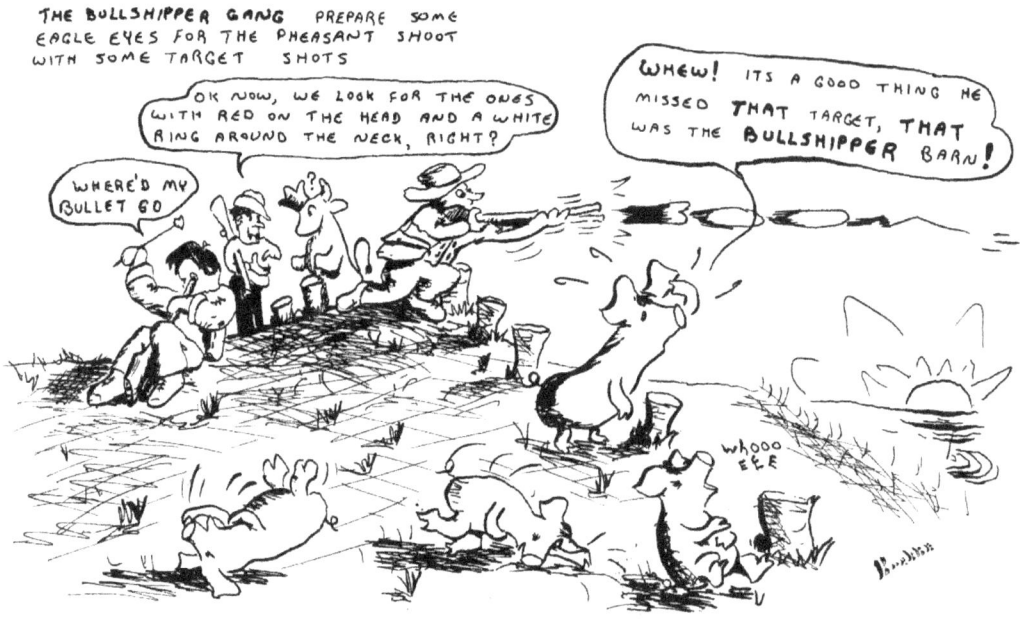

~ October 31, 1979

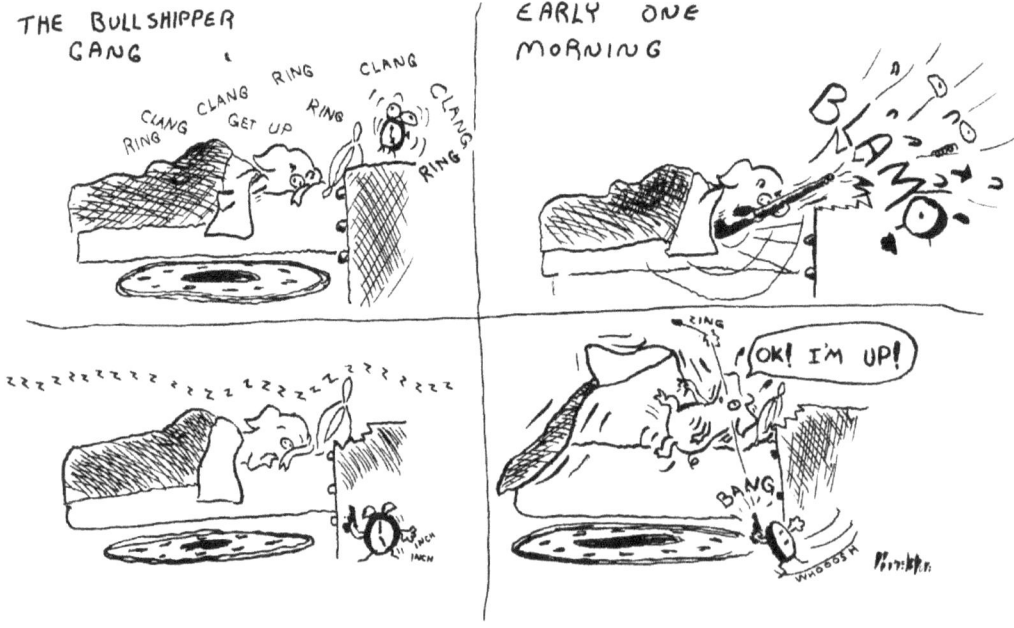

~ November 7, 14, 1979

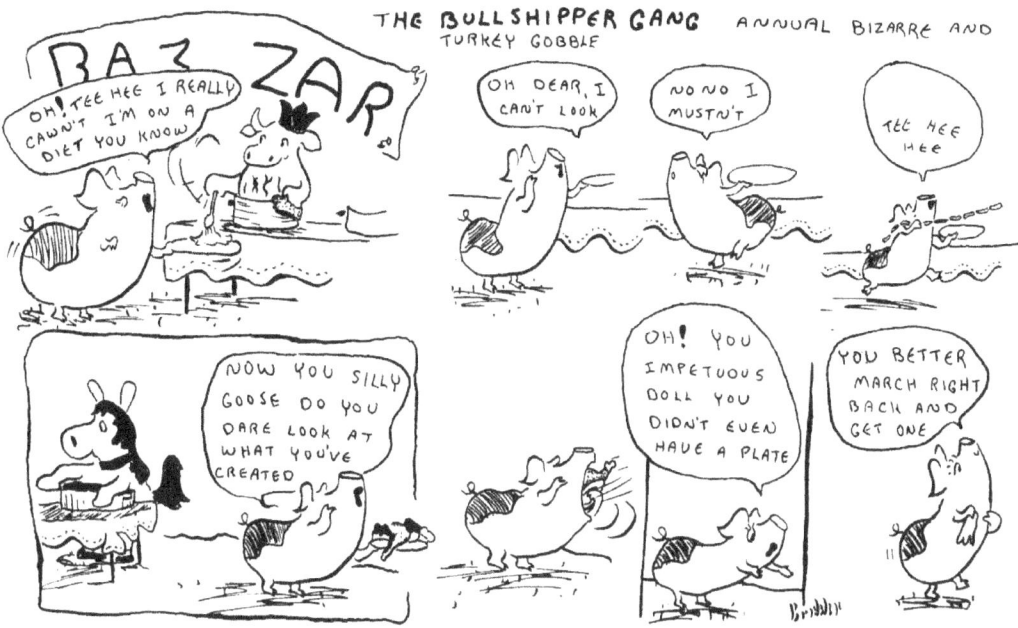

~ November 21, 1979

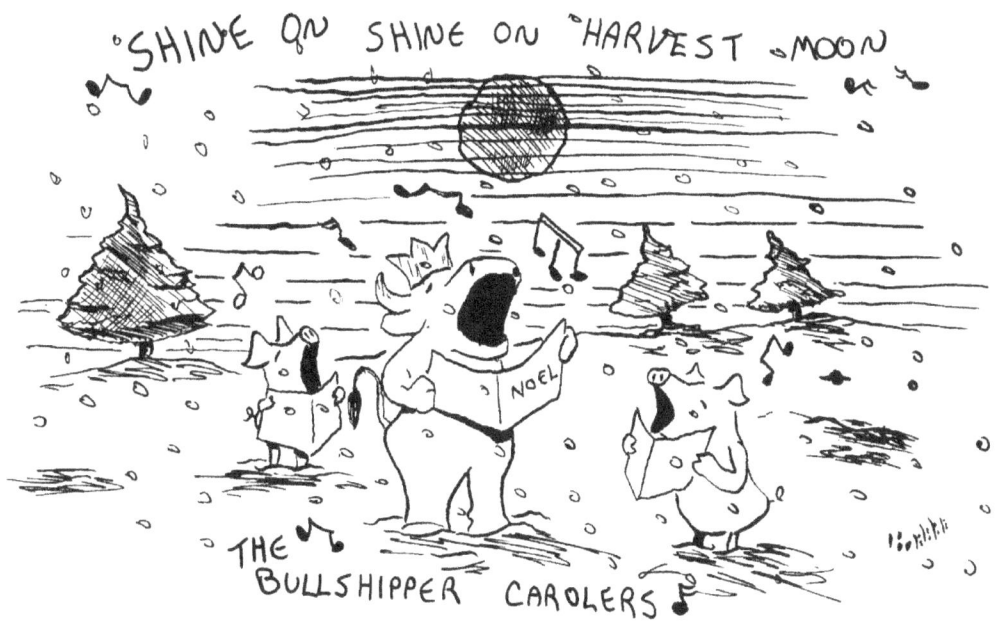

~ November 28, 1979

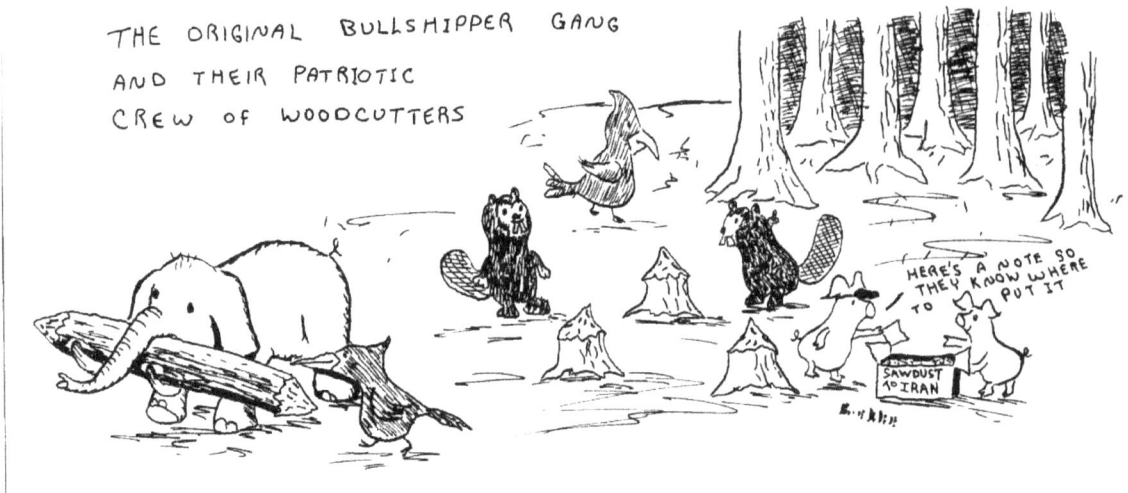

~ December 5, 1979

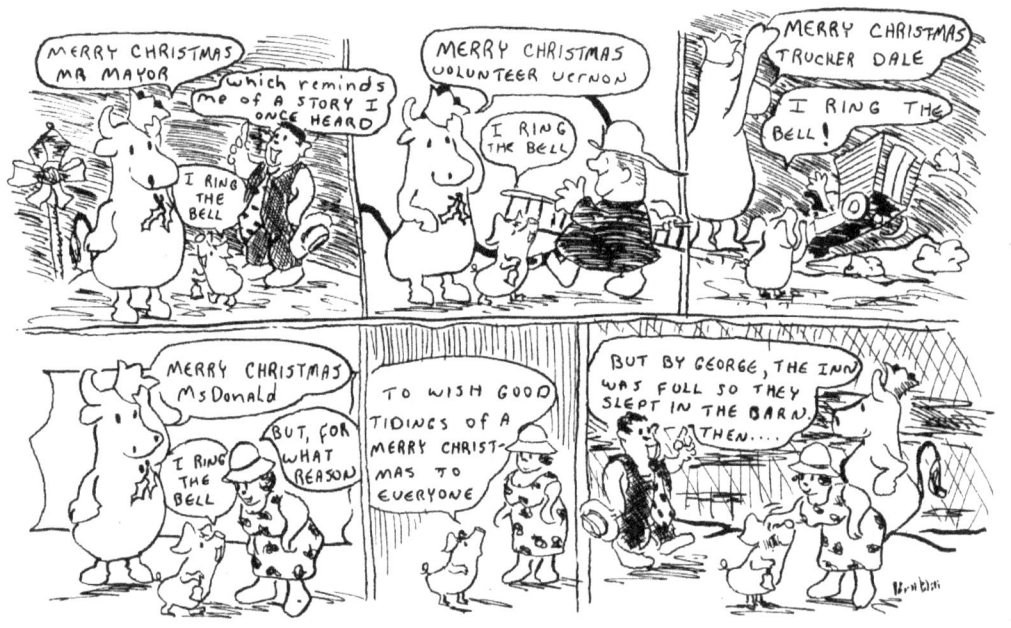

~ December 12, 1979

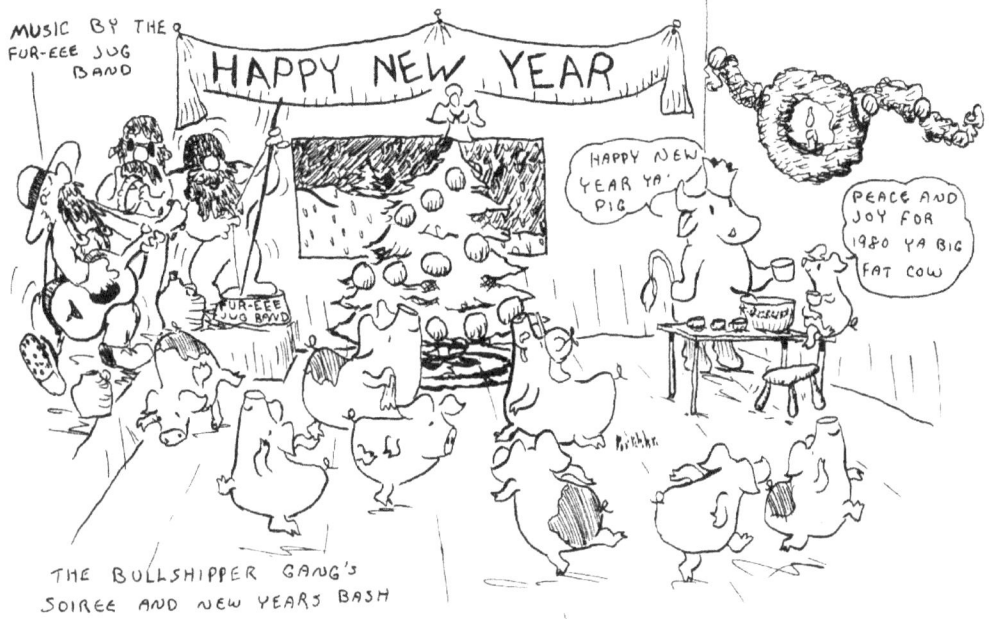

~ December 19, 1979

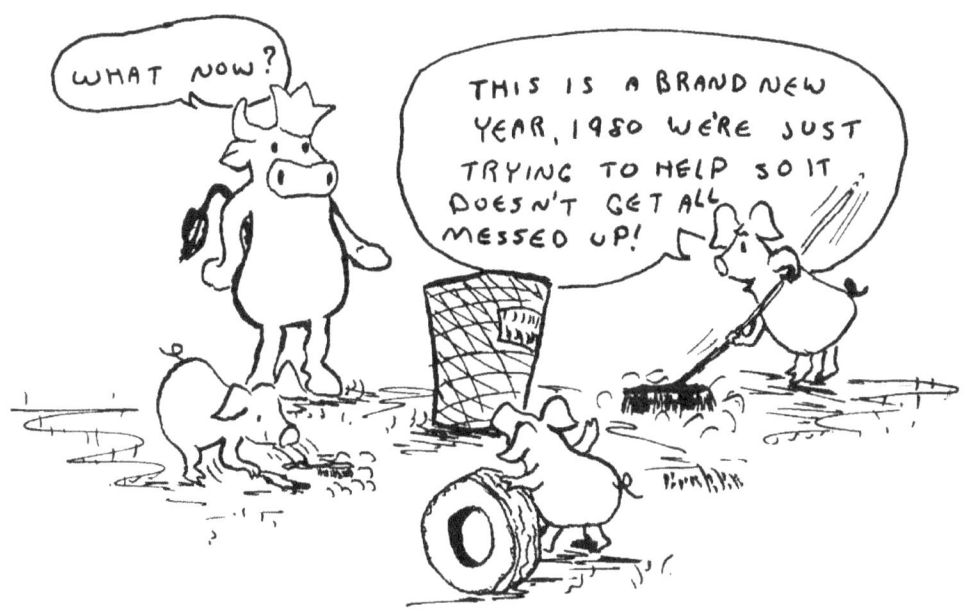

~ December 26, 1979

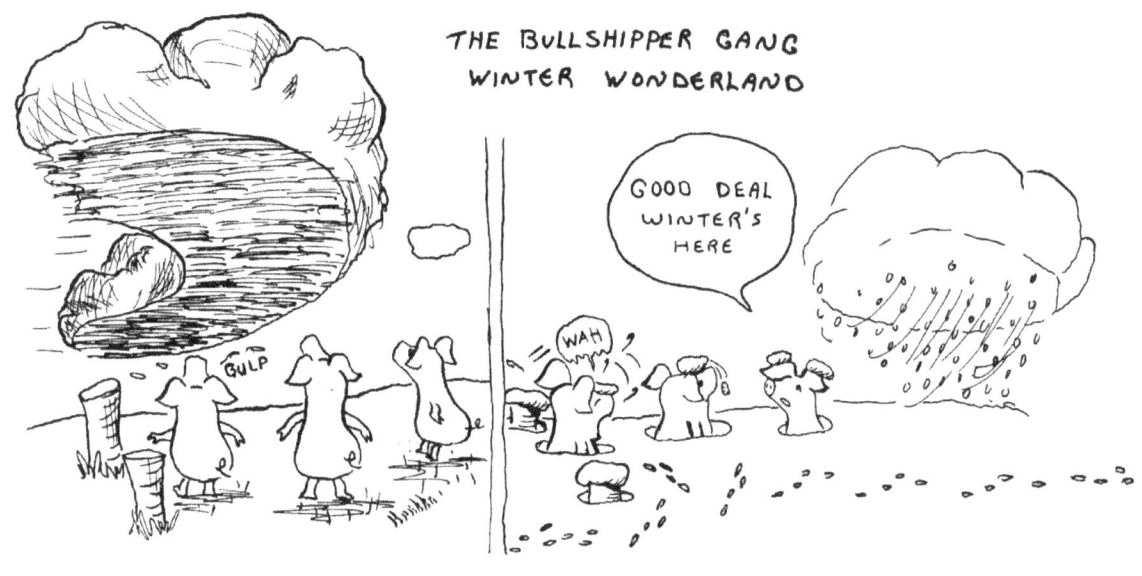

~ January 2, 9, 1980

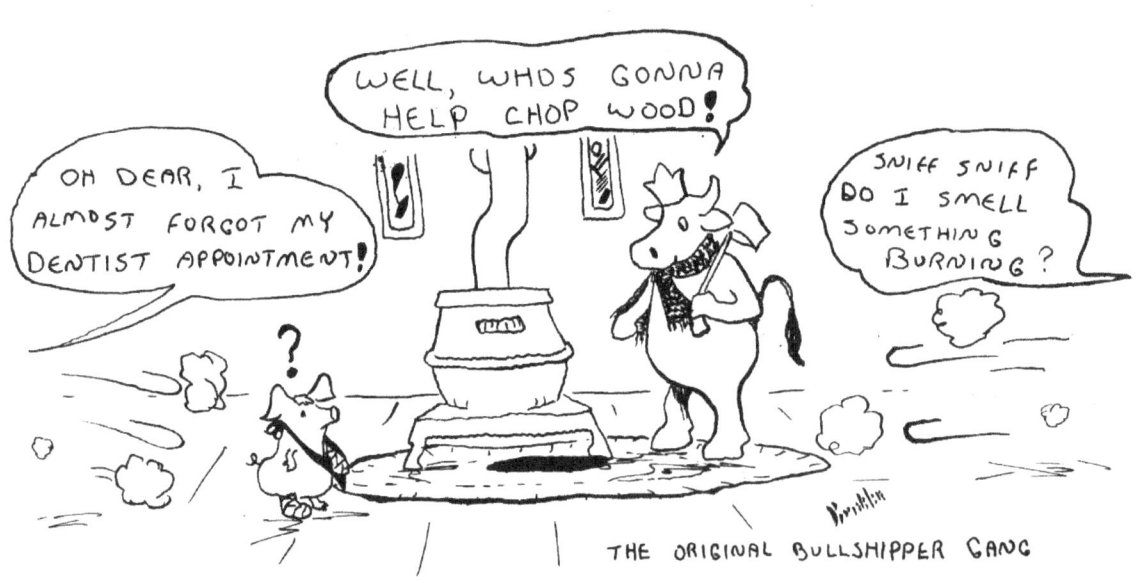

~ January 16, 1980

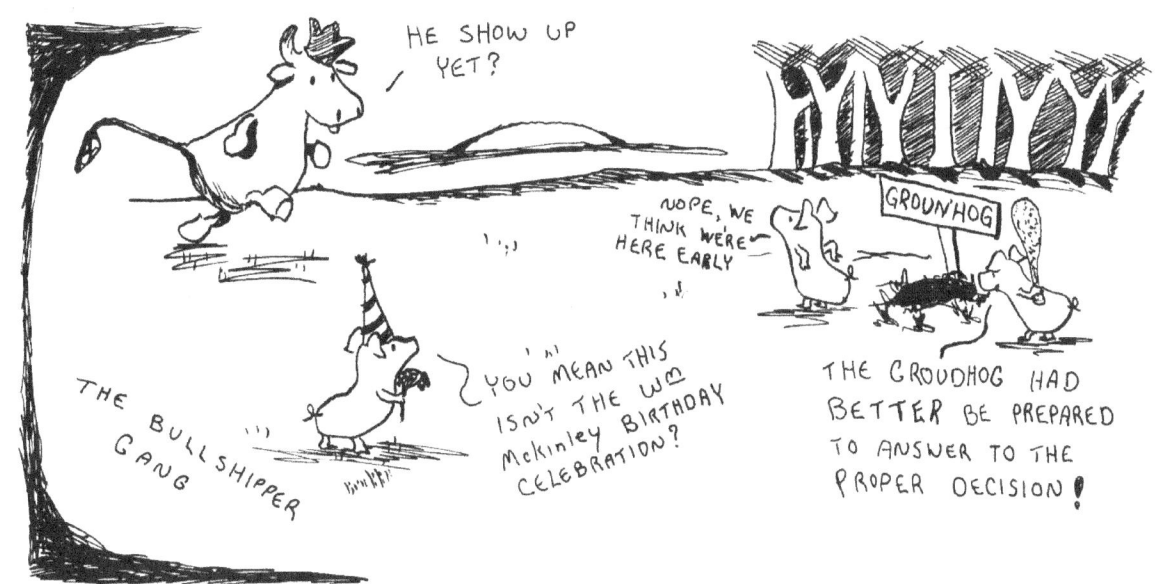

~ January 23, 1980

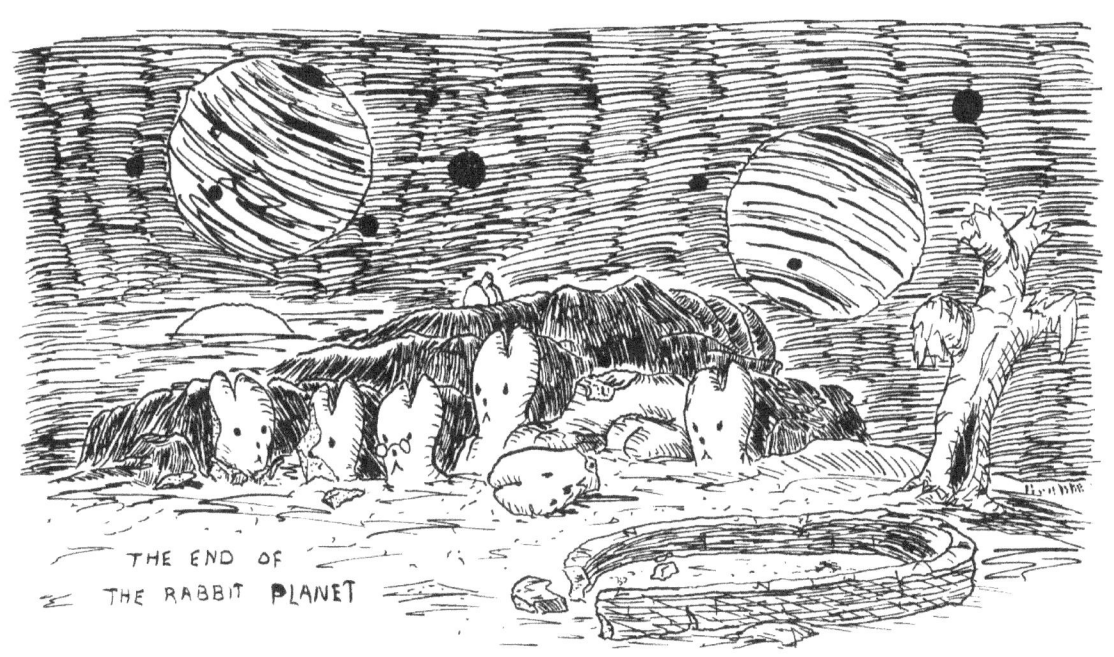

~ January 30, 1980

Don now lives in his new home and you may call him at 985-4079.

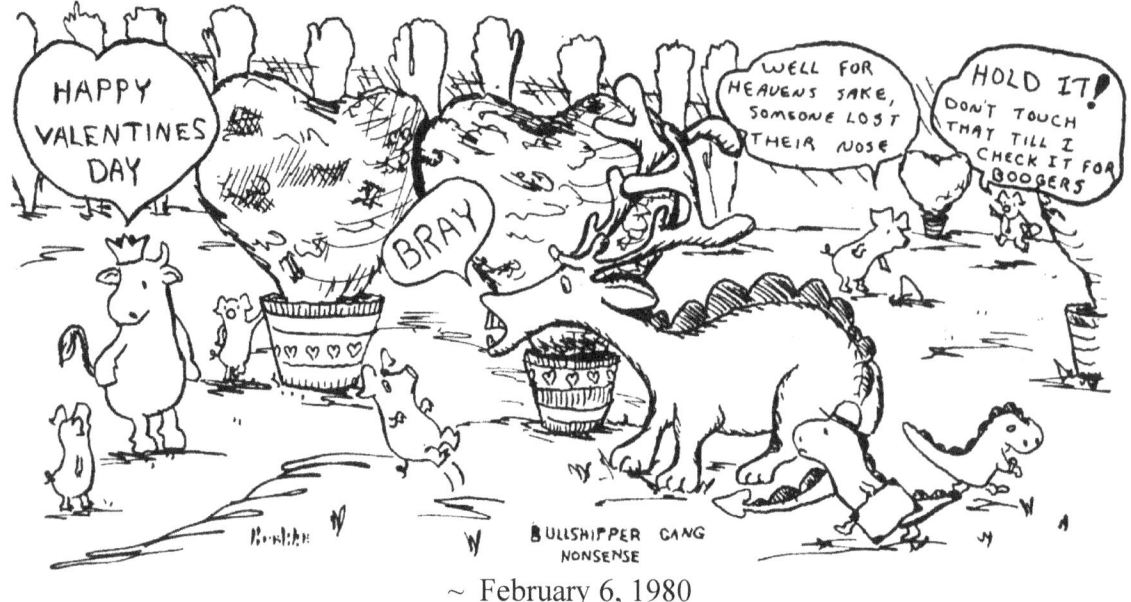

~ February 6, 1980

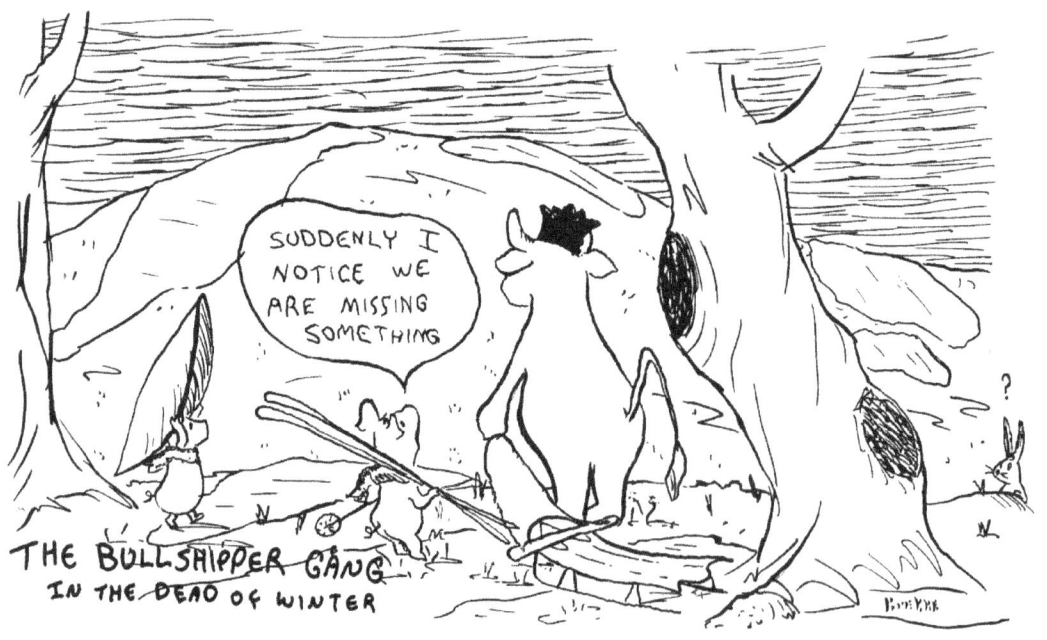

~ February 13, 1980

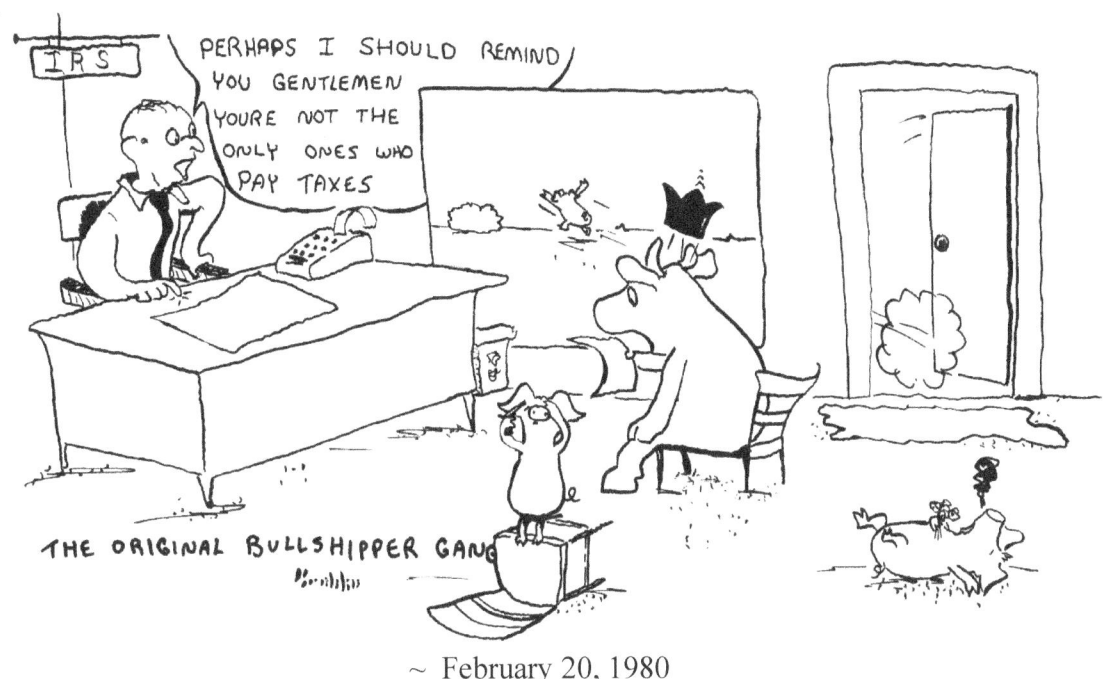

~ February 20, 1980

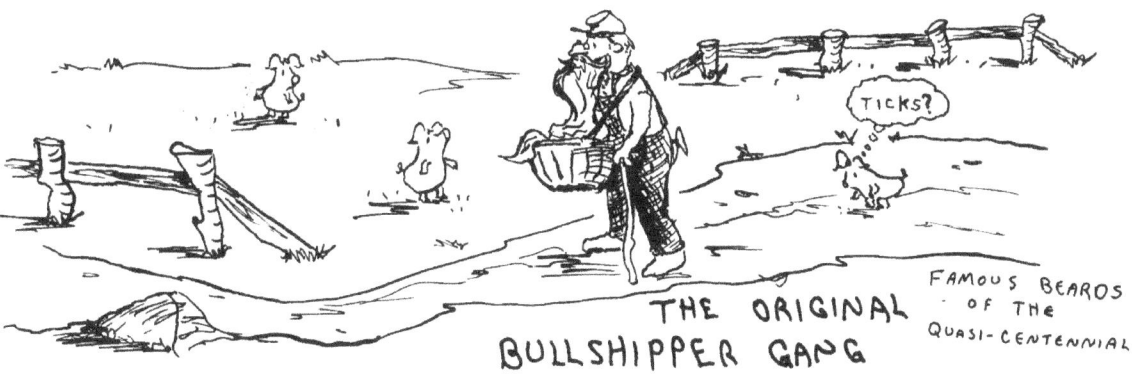

~ February 27, 1980

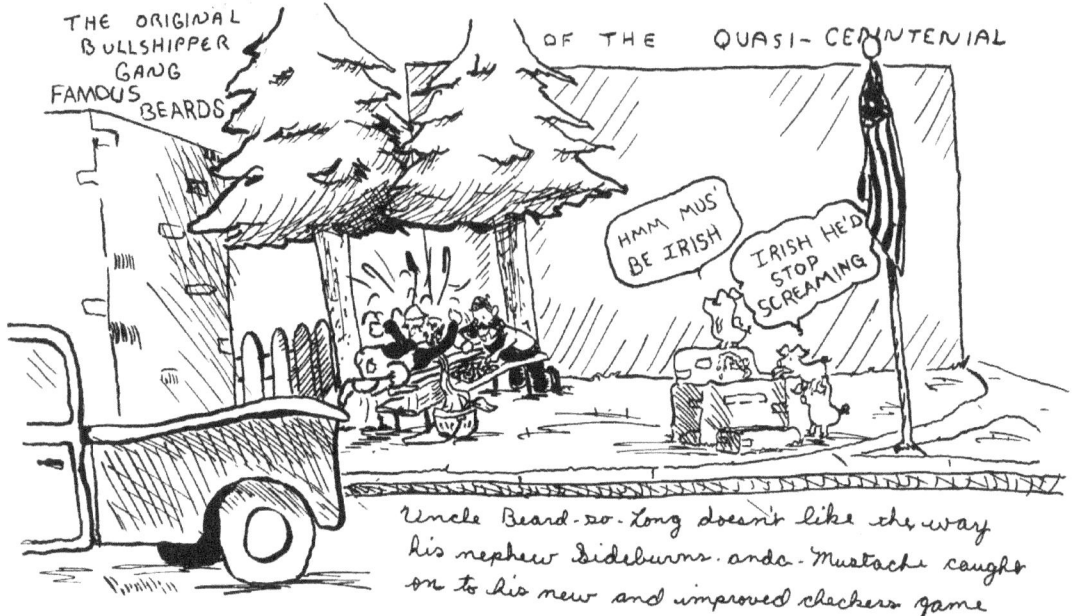

Uncle Beard-so-Long doesn't like the way his nephew Sideburns-and-a-Mustache caught on to his new and improved checkers game

~ March 5, 1980

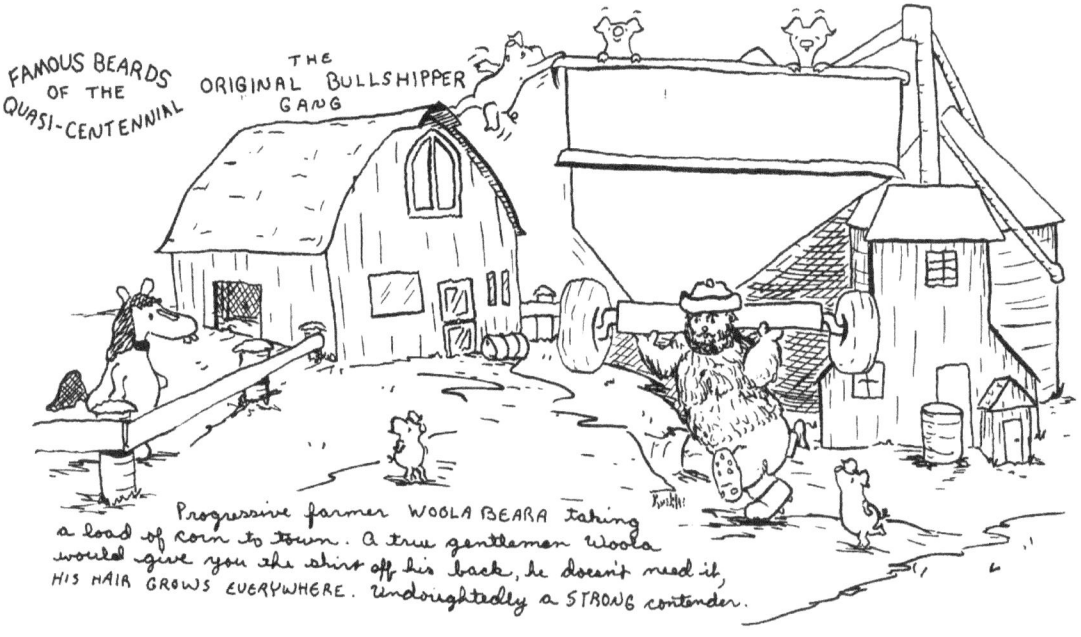

Progressive farmer WOOLA BEARA taking a load of corn to town. A true gentleman Woola would give you the shirt off his back, he doesn't need it, HIS HAIR GROWS EVERYWHERE. Undoughtedly a STRONG contender.

~ March 12, 1980

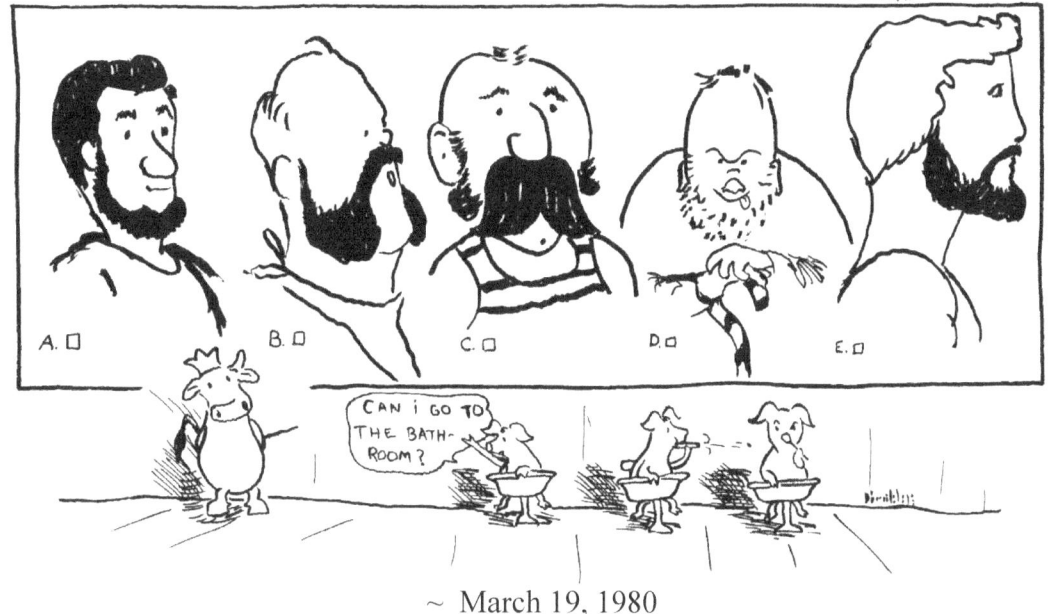

~ March 19, 1980

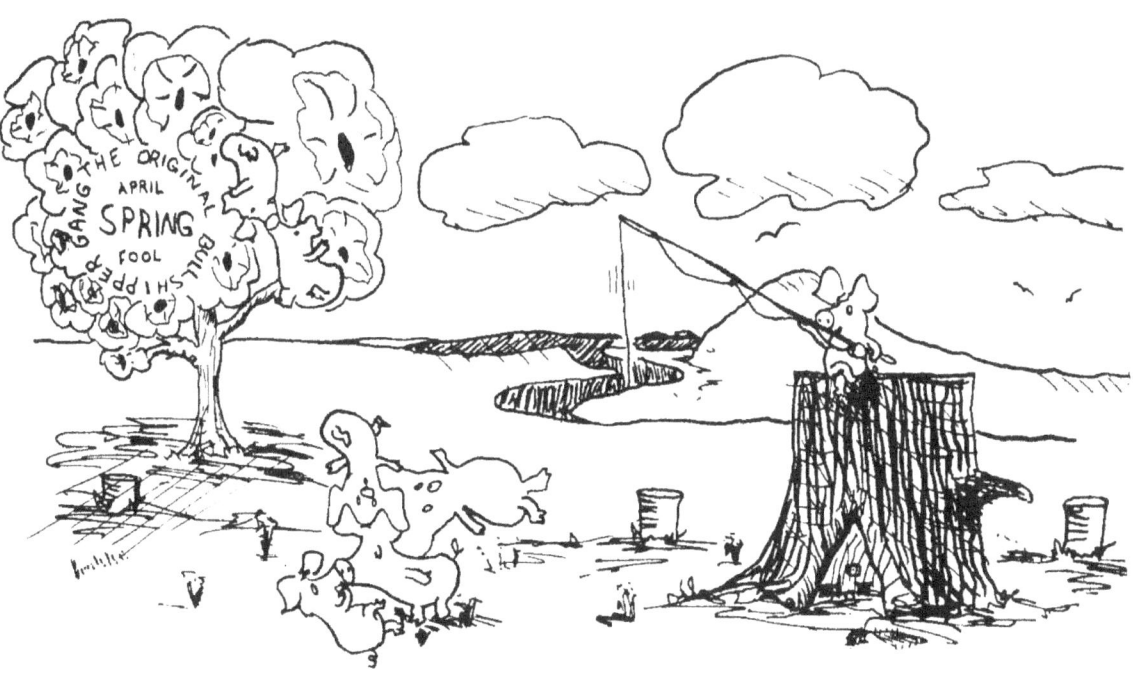

~ March 26, 1980

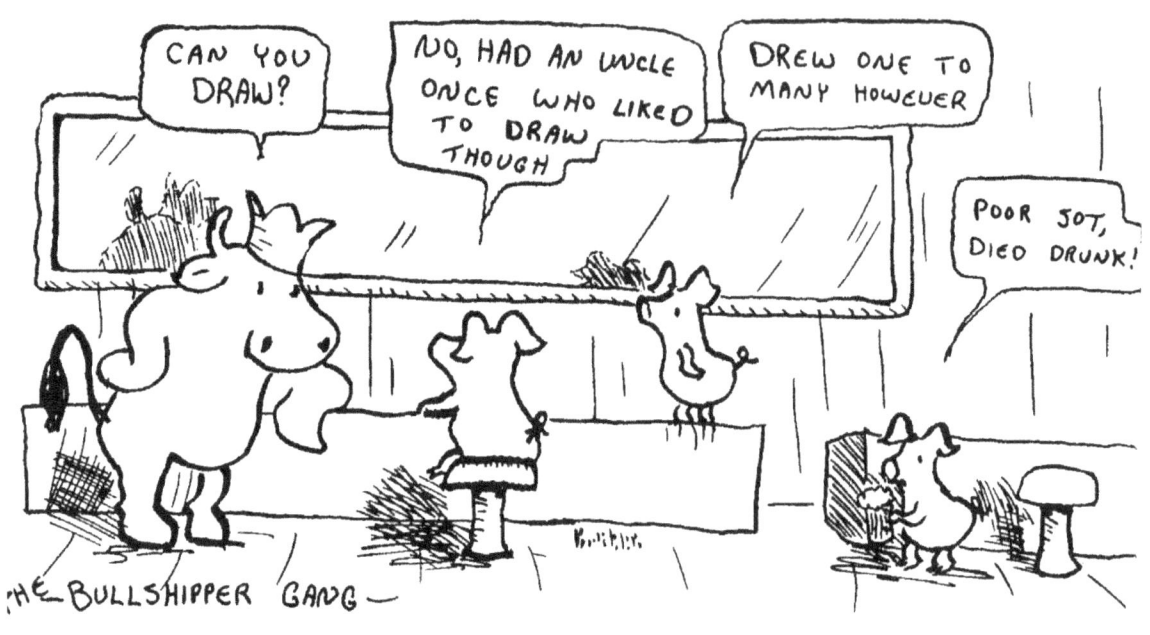

~ April 2, 1980

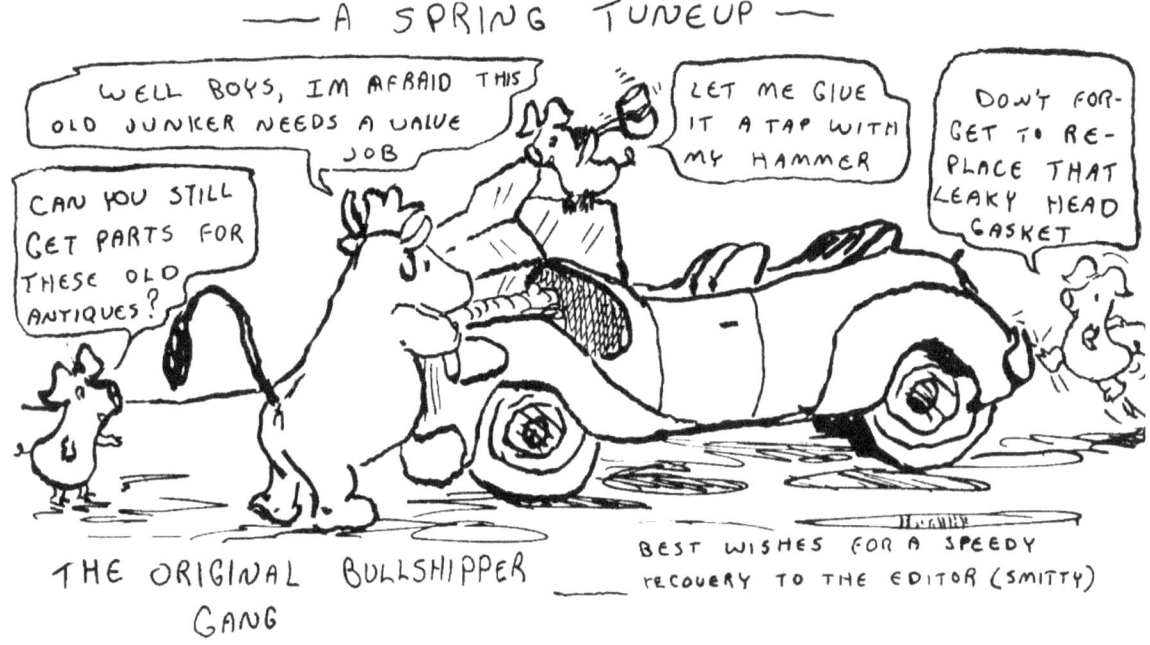

~ April 16, 1980

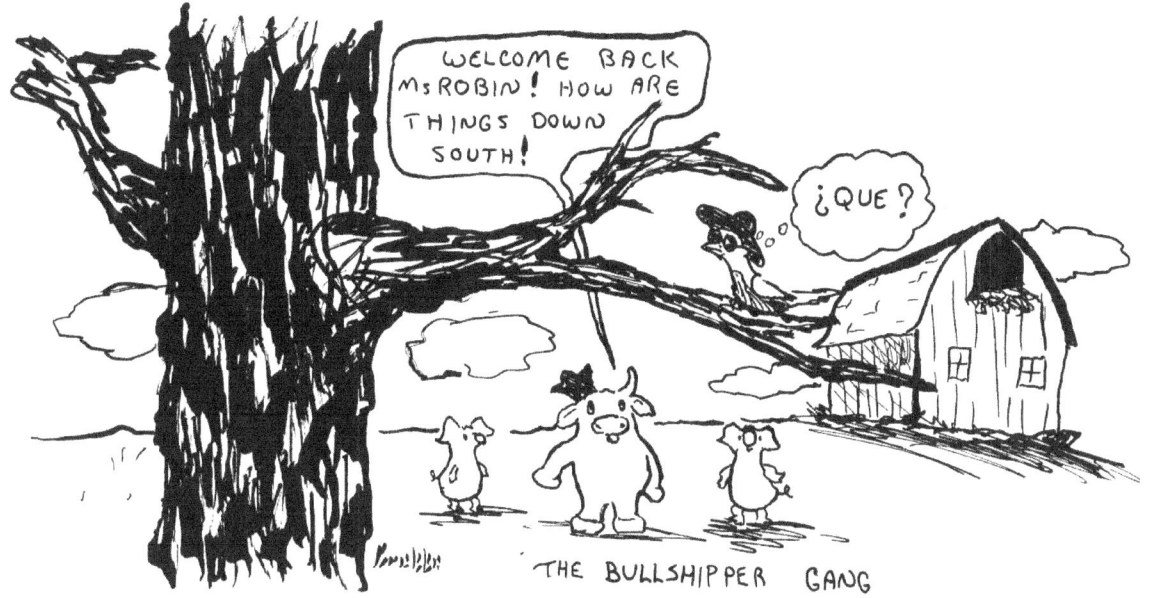

~ April 23, 1980

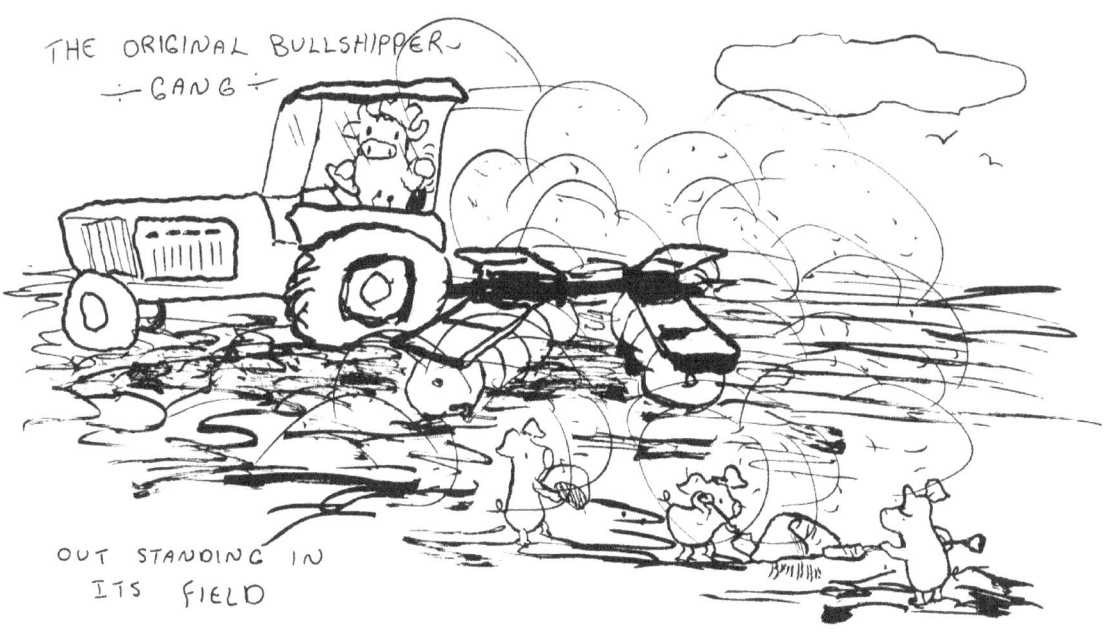

~ April 30, 1980

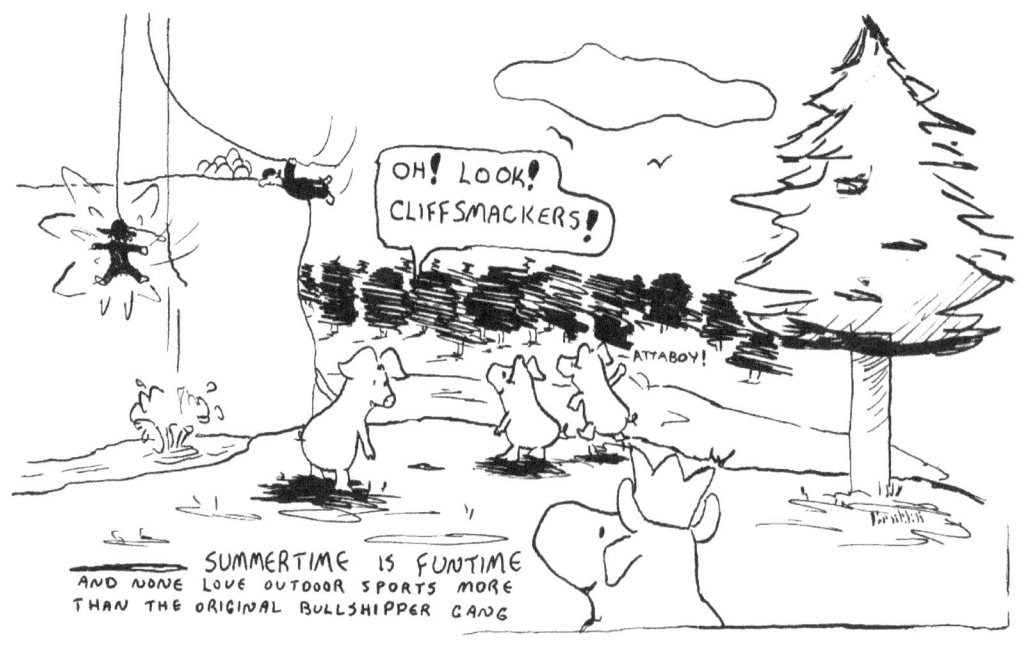

~ May 7, 1980

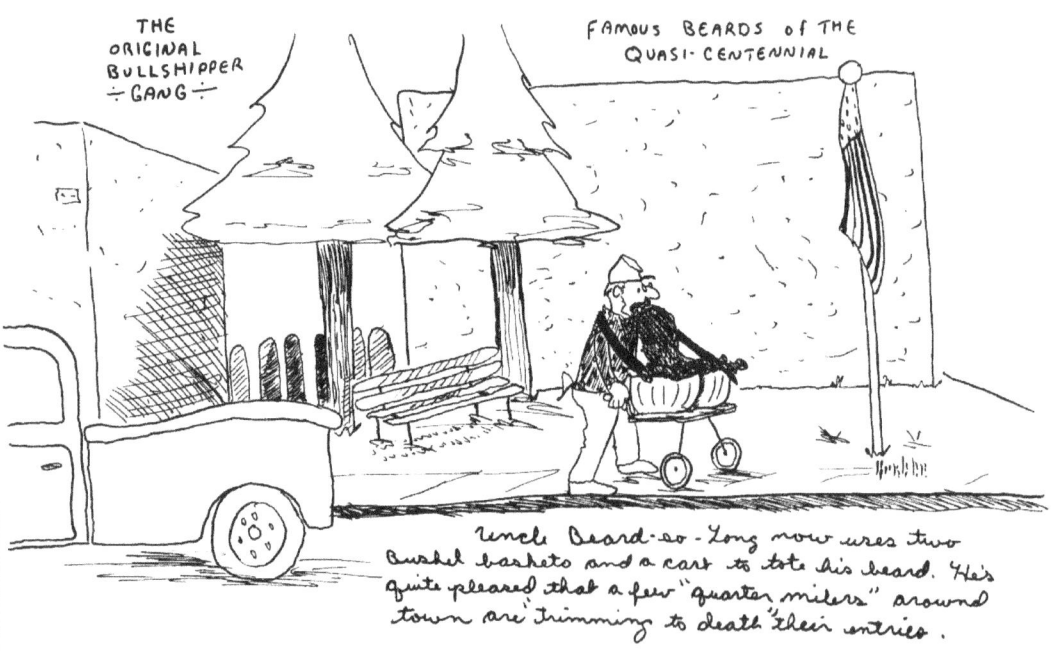

~ May 14, 1980

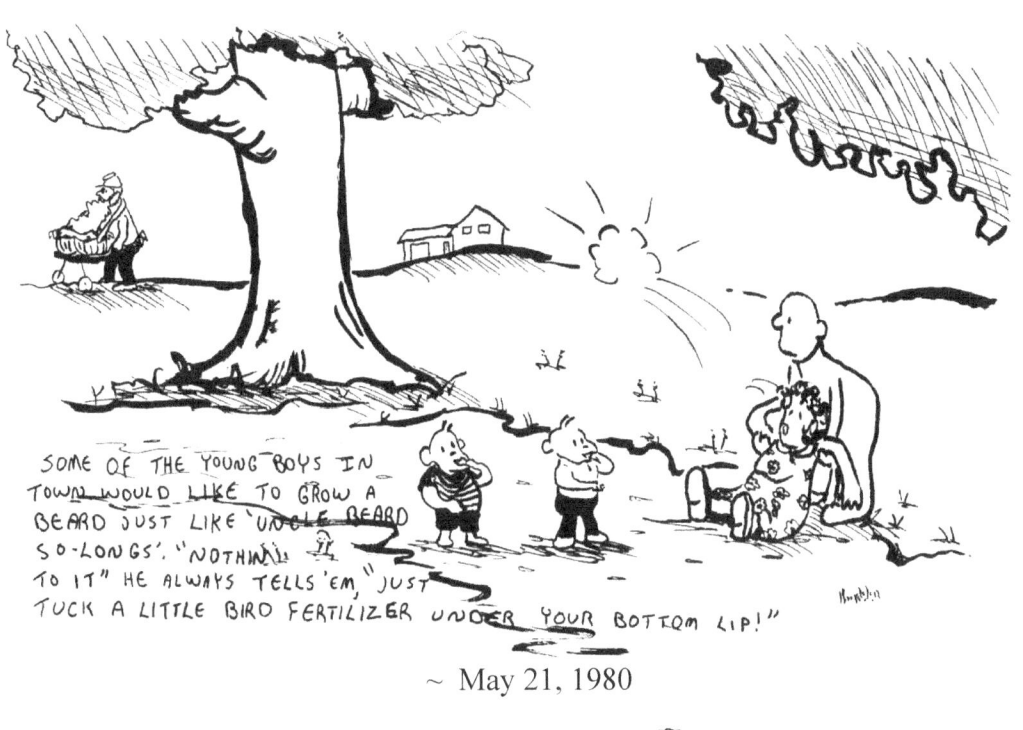

~ May 21, 1980

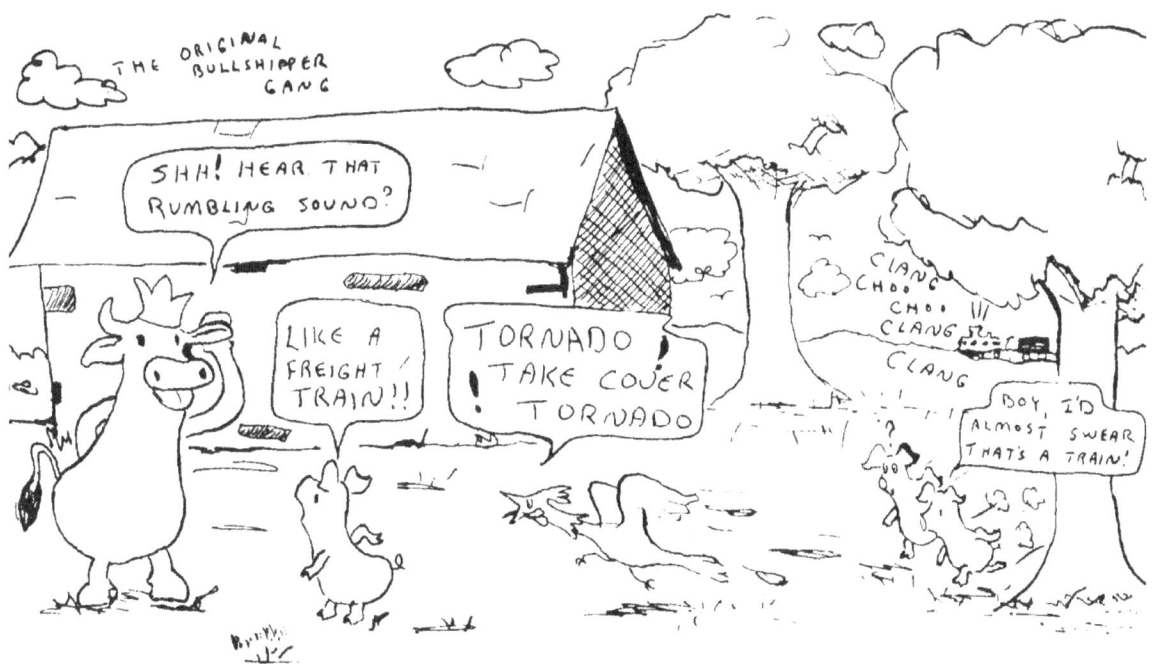

~ May 28, 1980

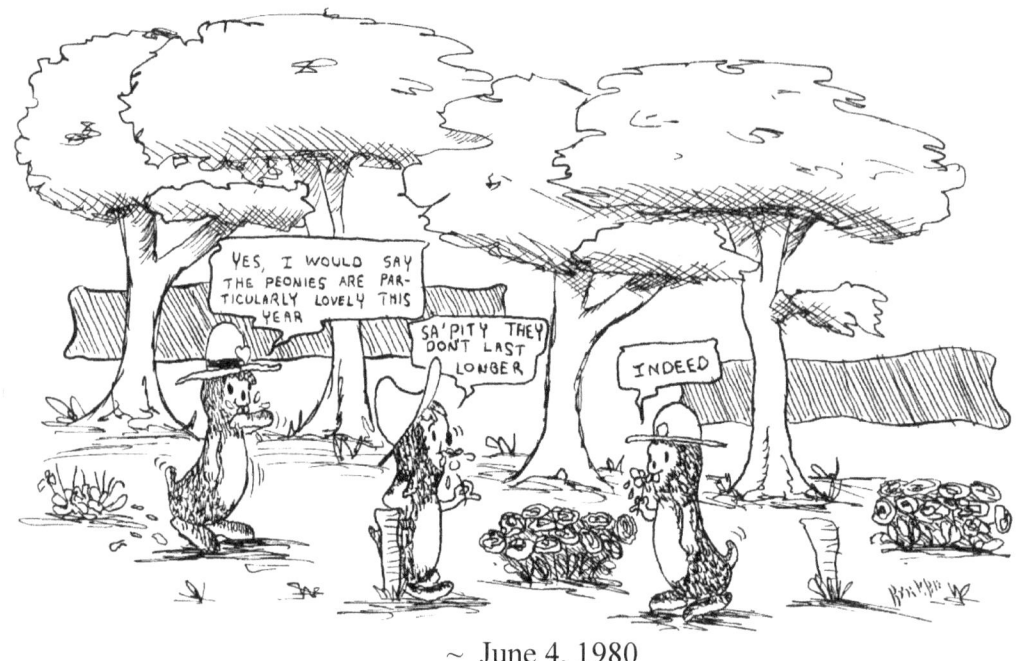

~ June 4, 1980

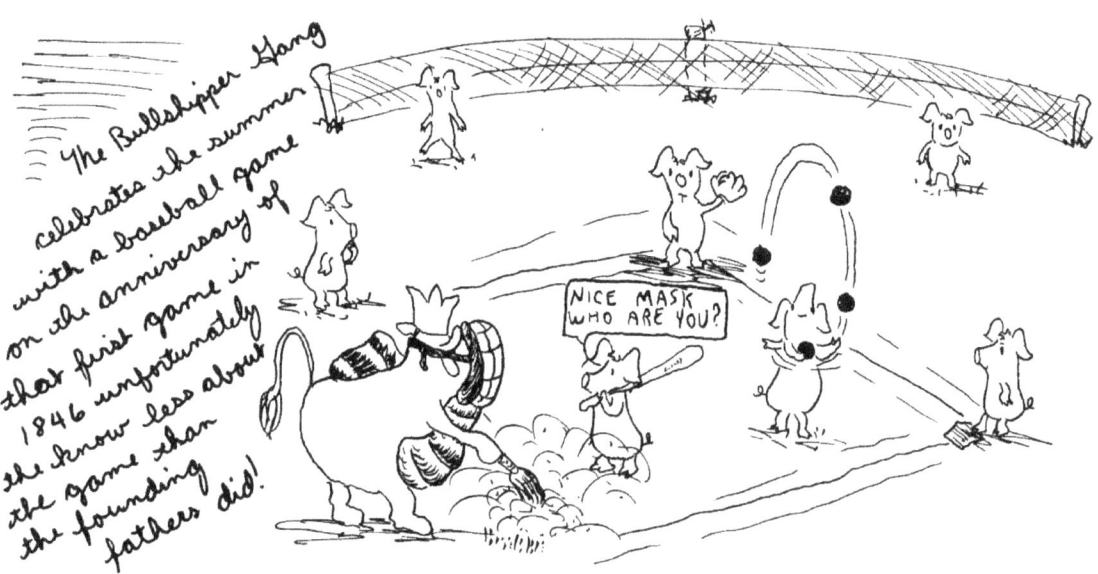

~ June 11, 1980

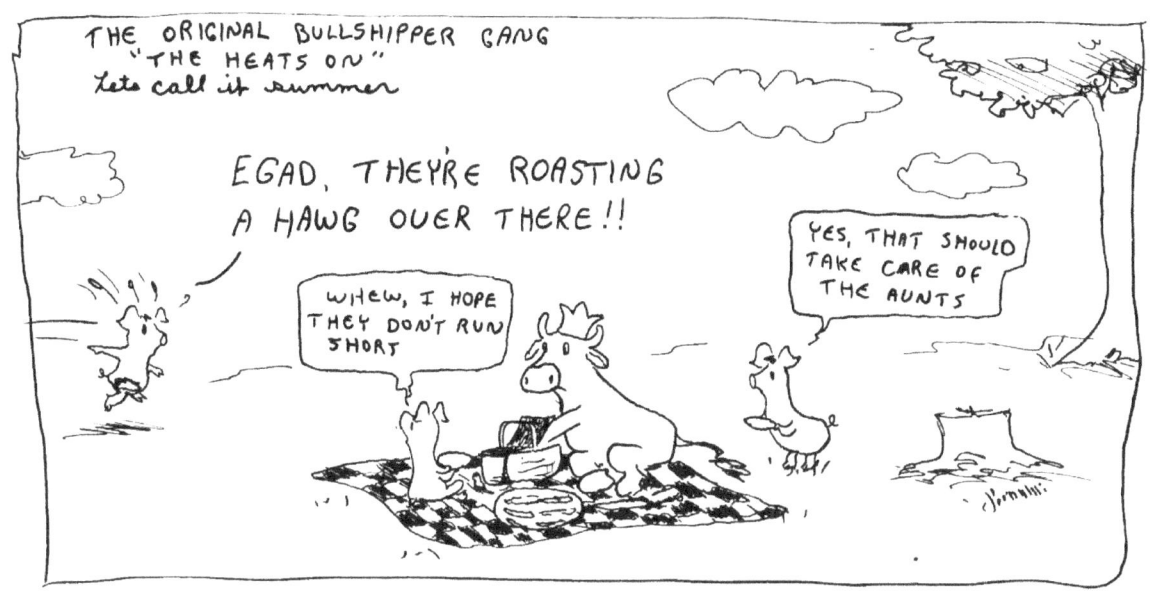

~ June 18, 1980

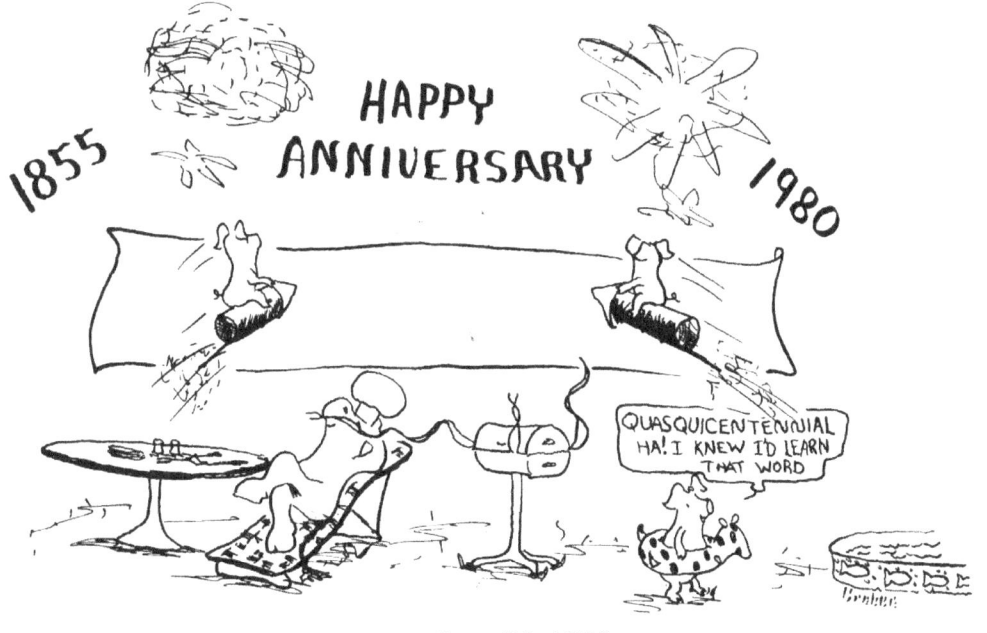

~ June 25, 1980

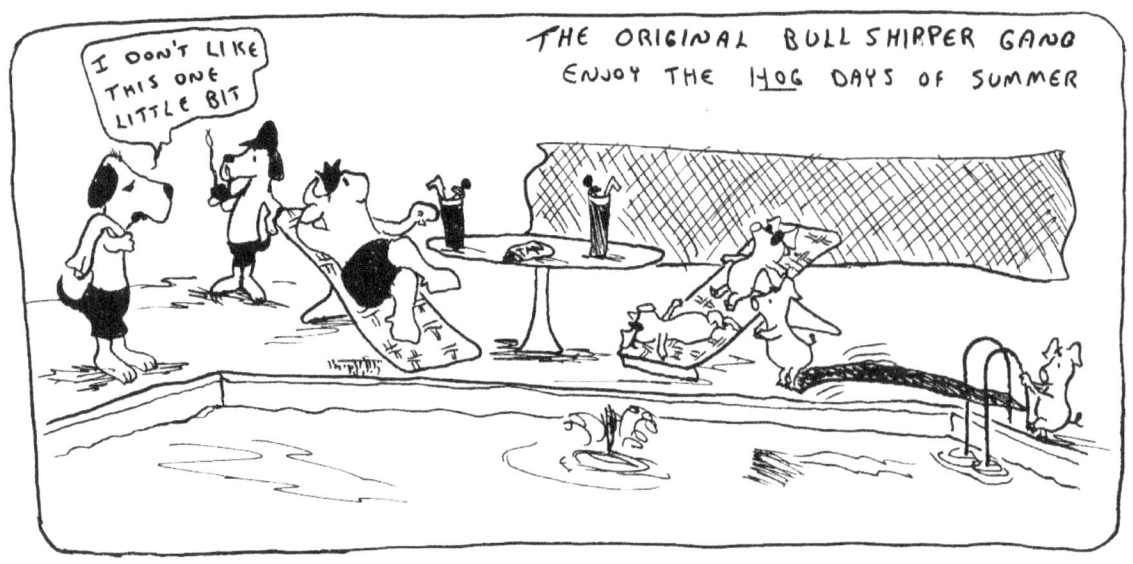

~ July 2, 1980

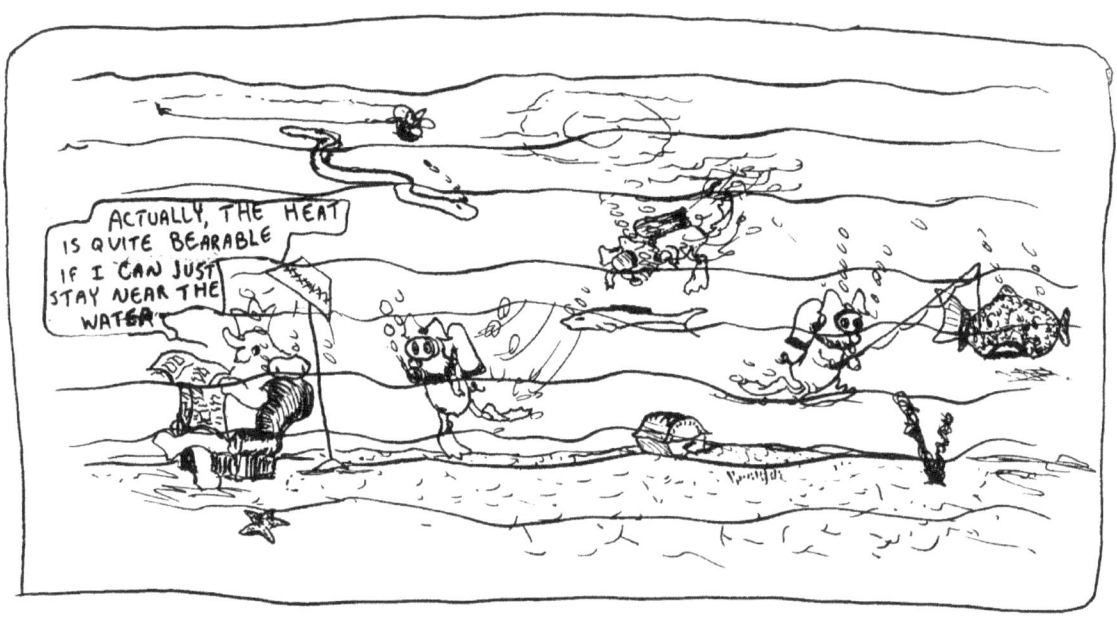

~ July 9, 1980

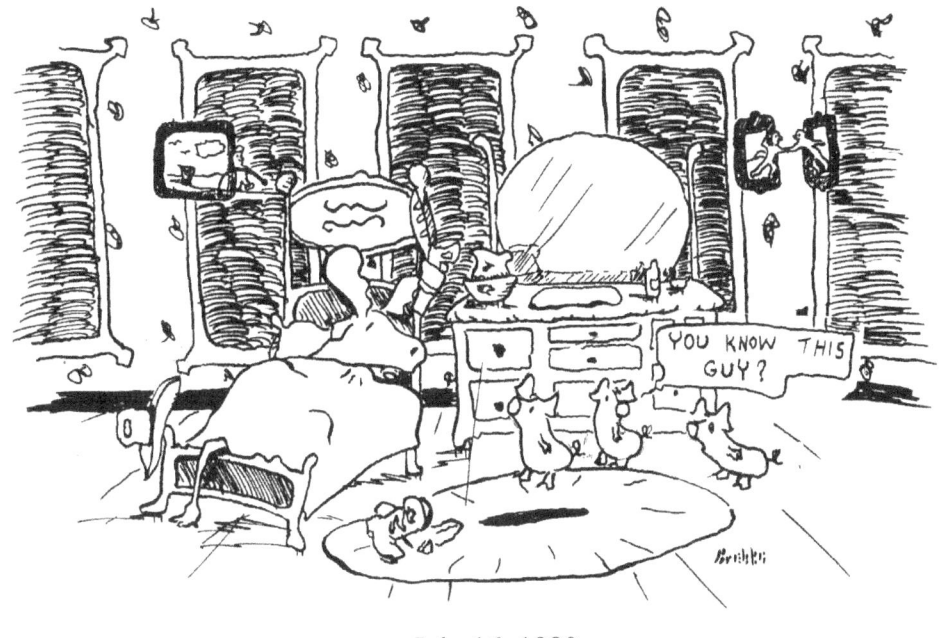

~ July 16, 1980

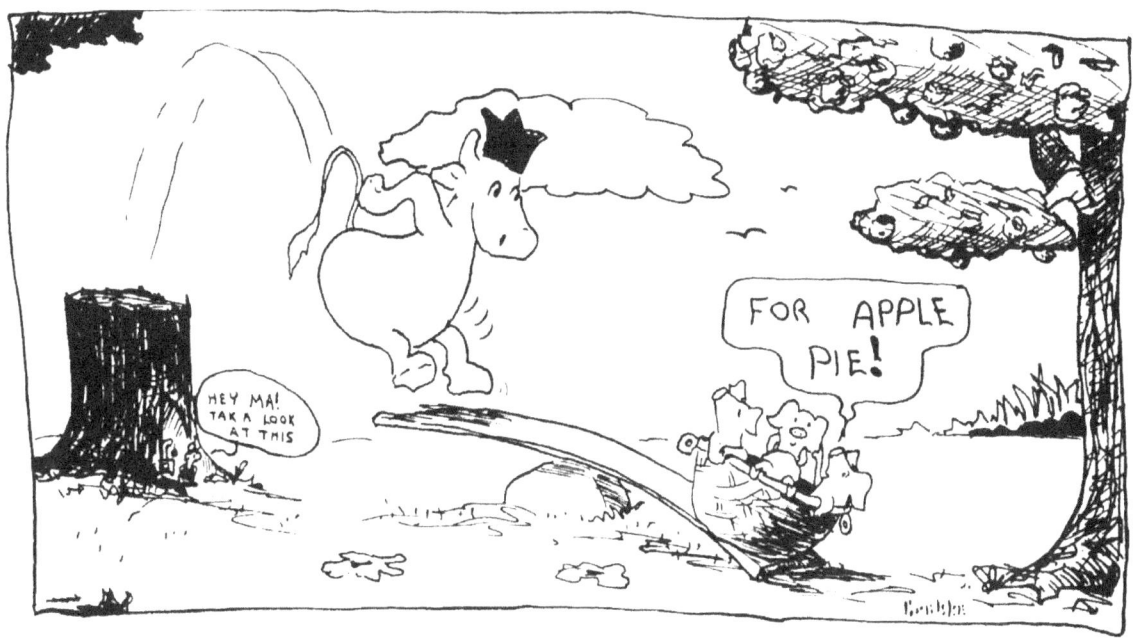

~ July 23, 1980

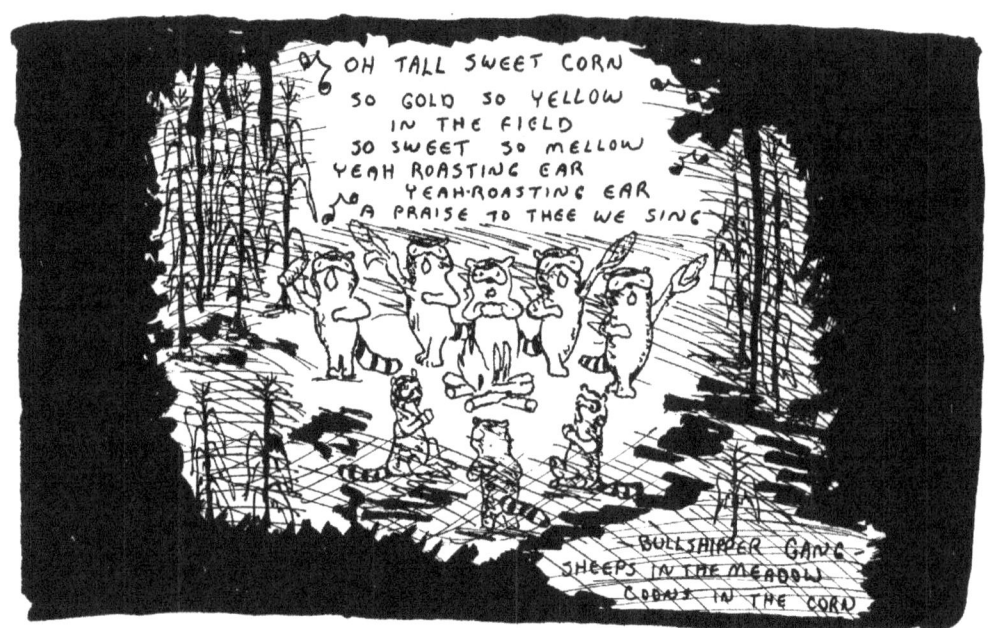

~ July 30, 1980

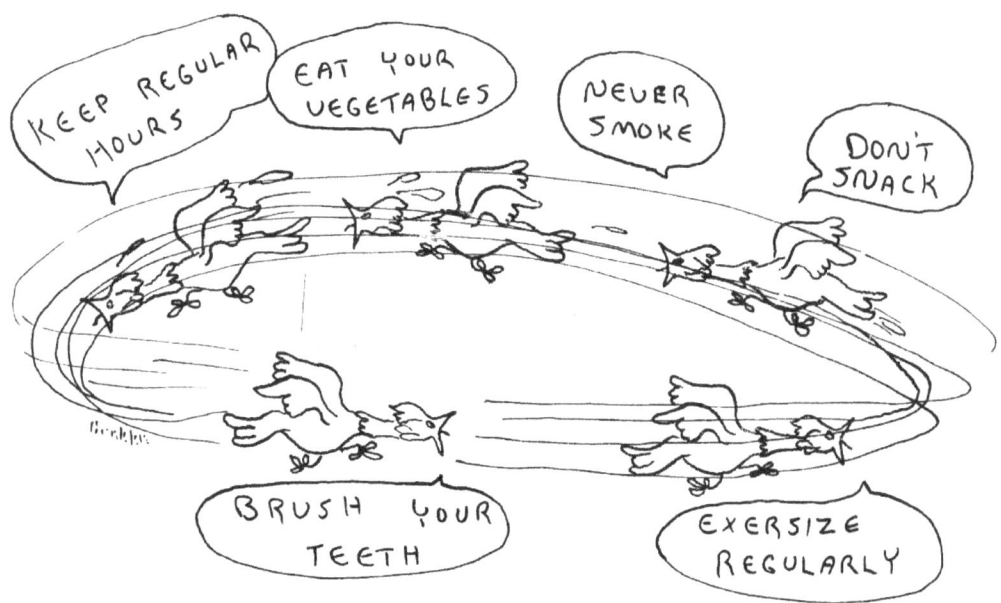

~ August 6, 1980

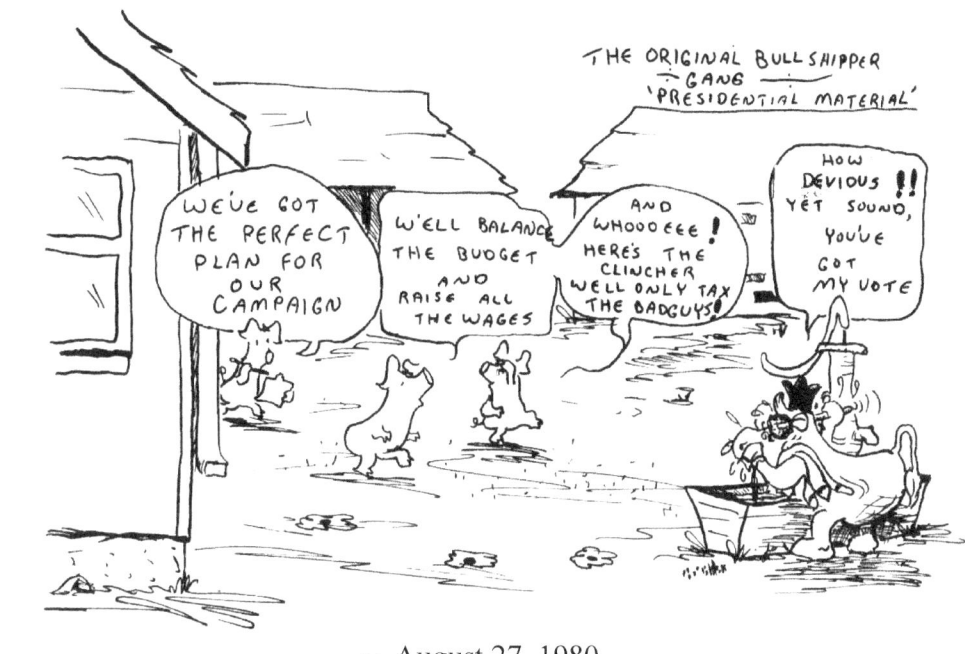

~ August 27, 1980

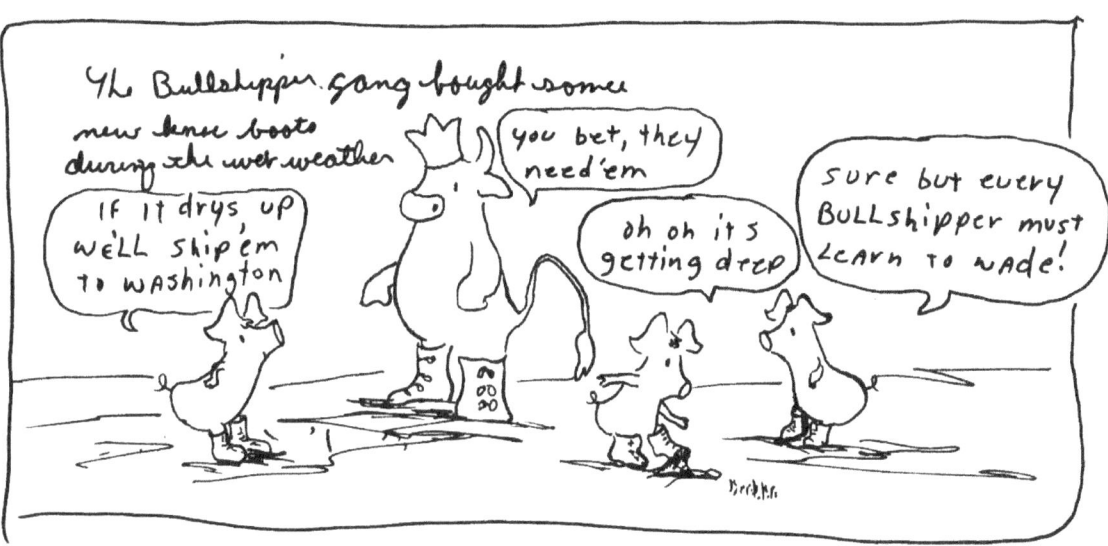

~ September 3, 1980

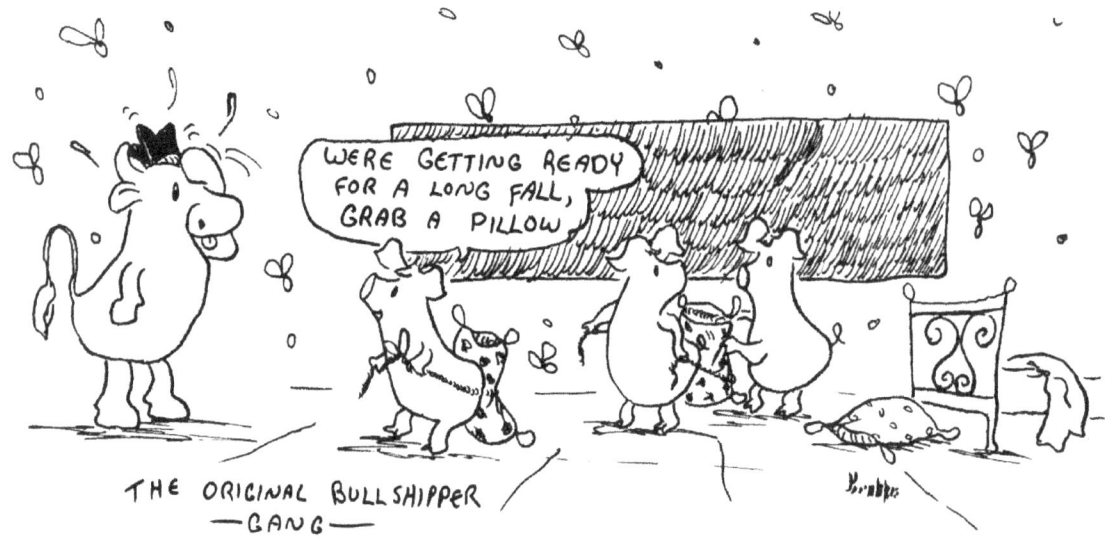

~ September 10, 17, 1980

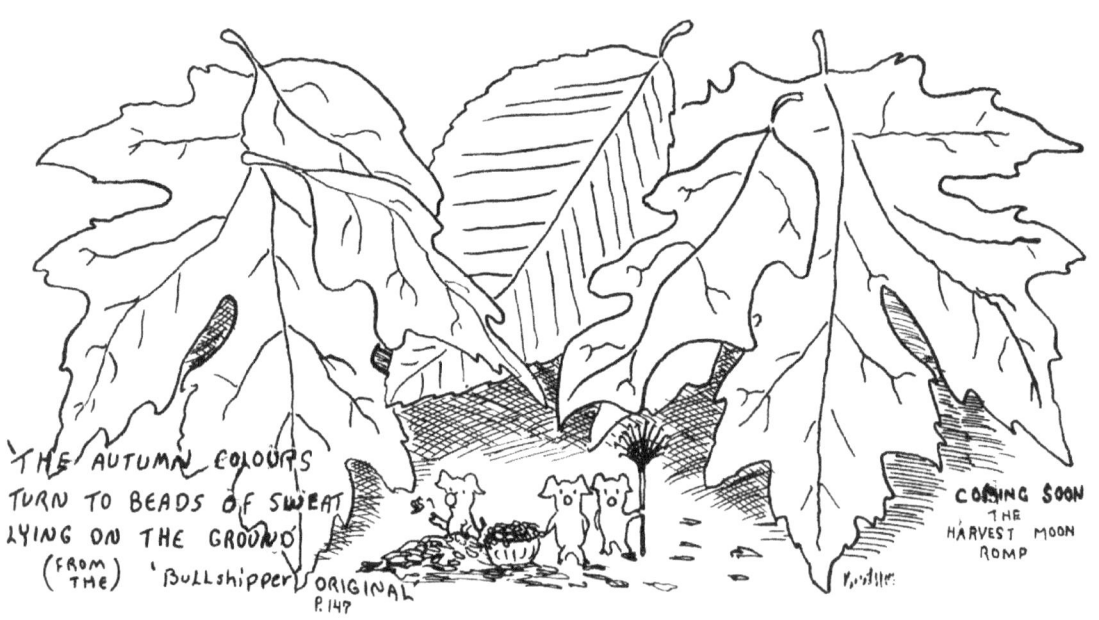

~ September 24, October 1, 1980

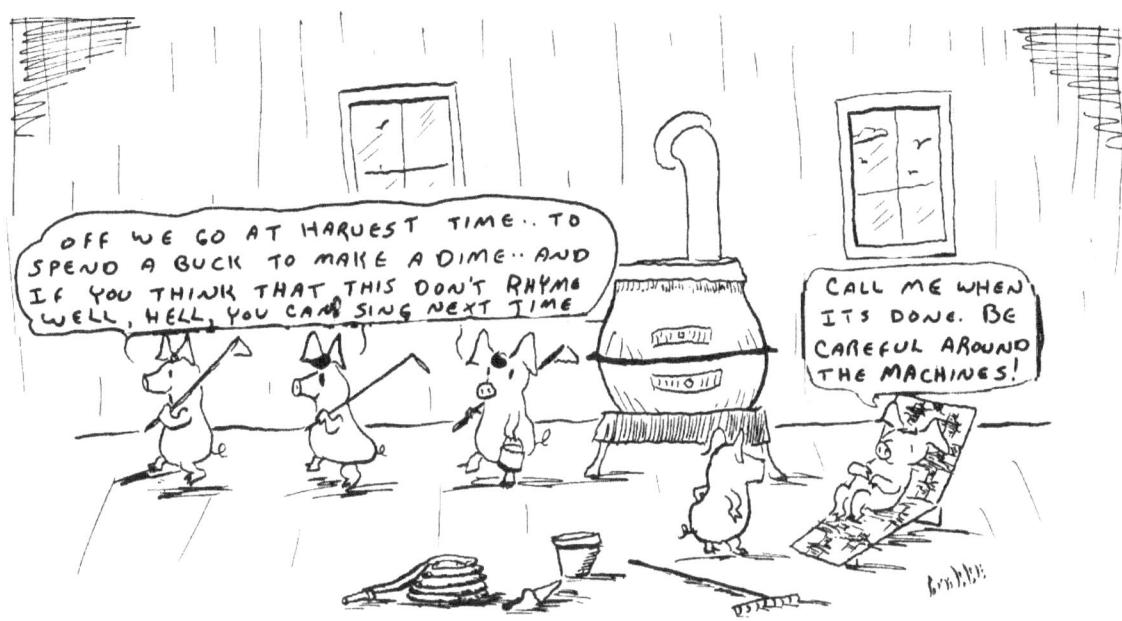

~ October 8, 1980

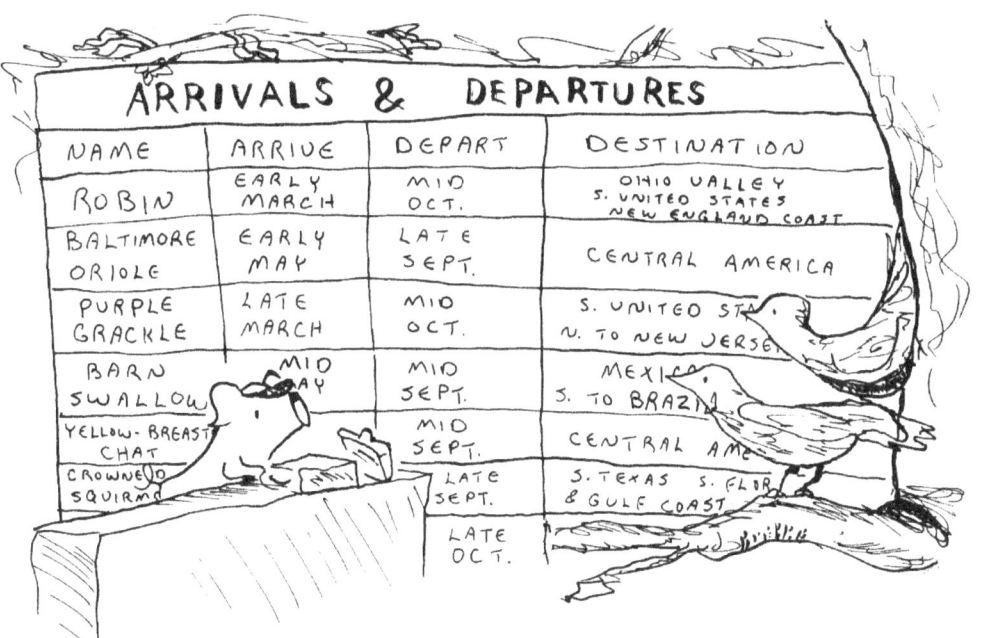

~ October 15, 22, 29, 1980

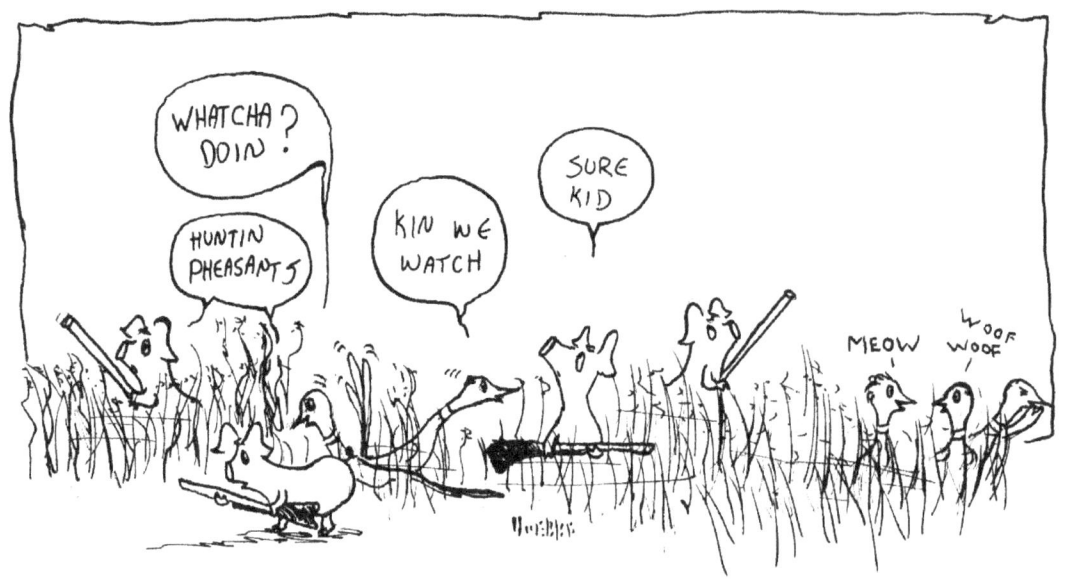

~ November 5, 1980

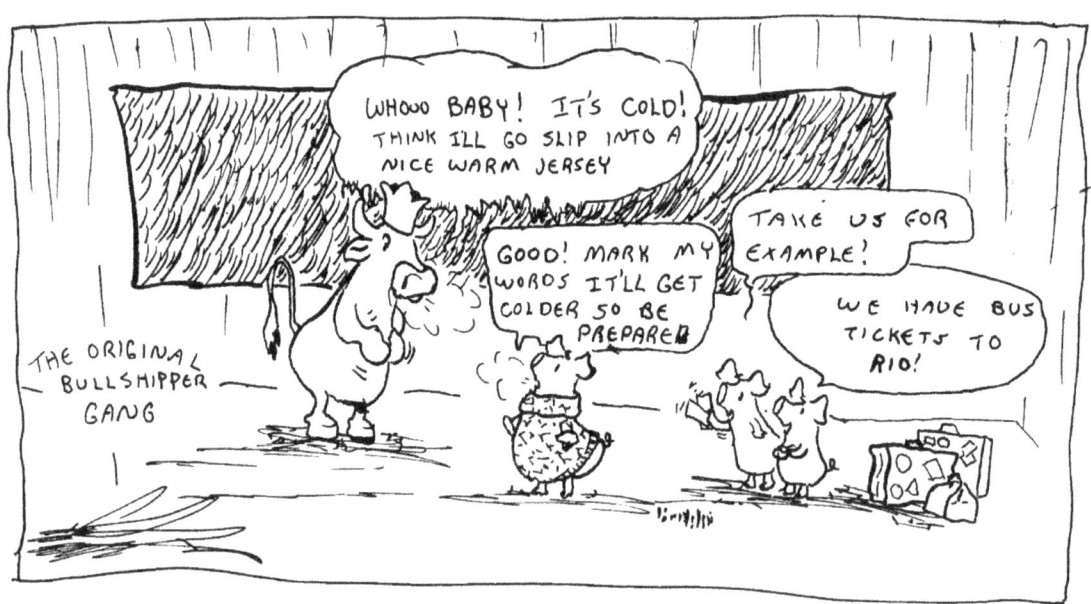

~ November 12, 19, 1980

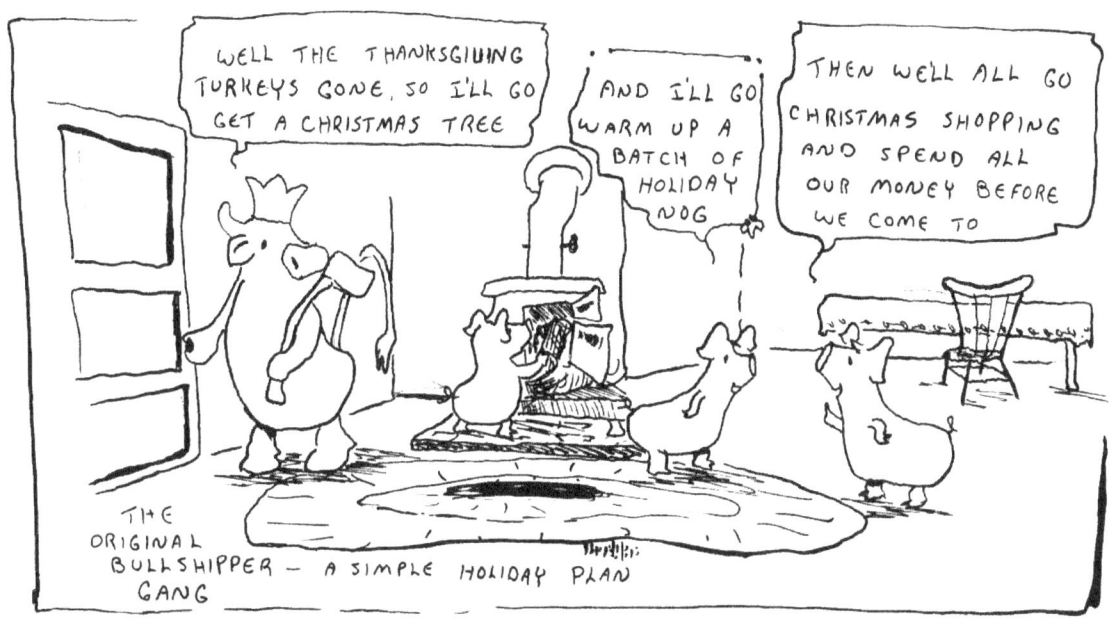

~ November 26, 1980

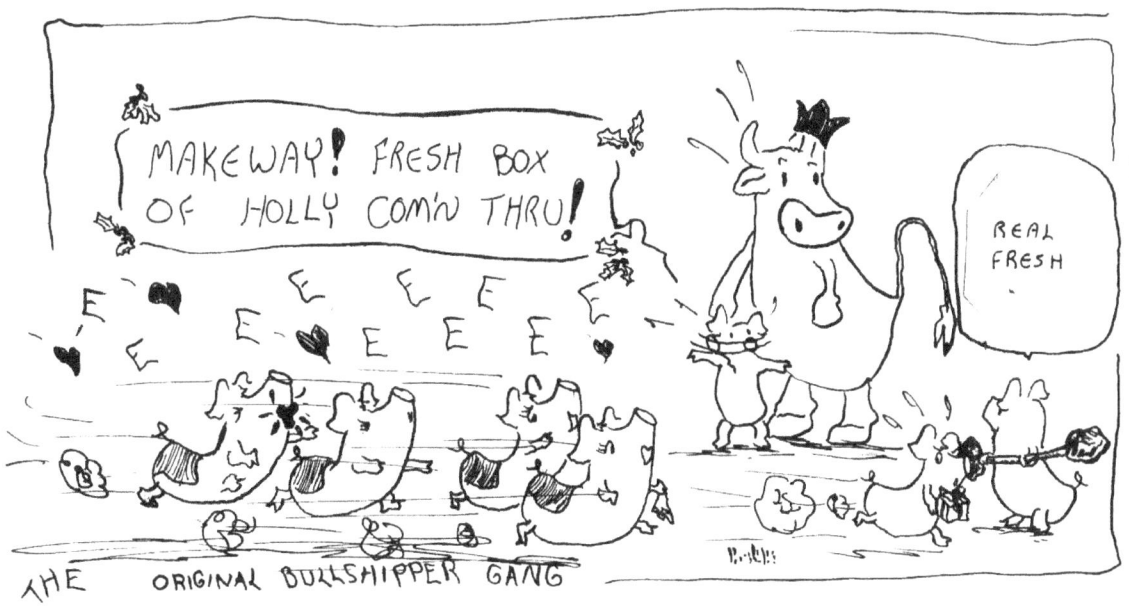

~ December 3, 1980

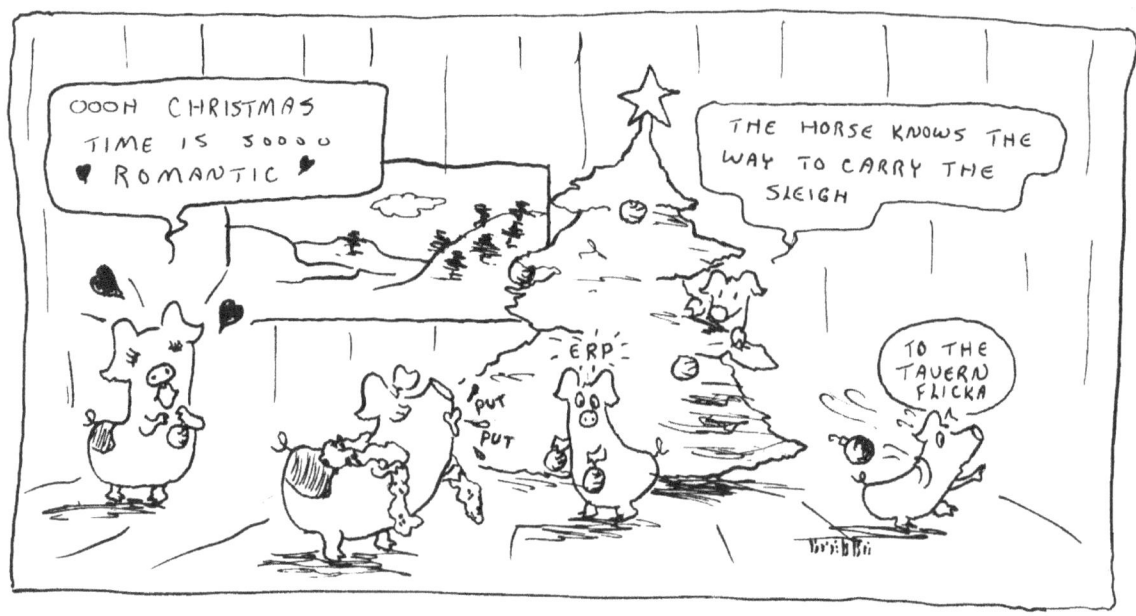

~ December 17, 1980

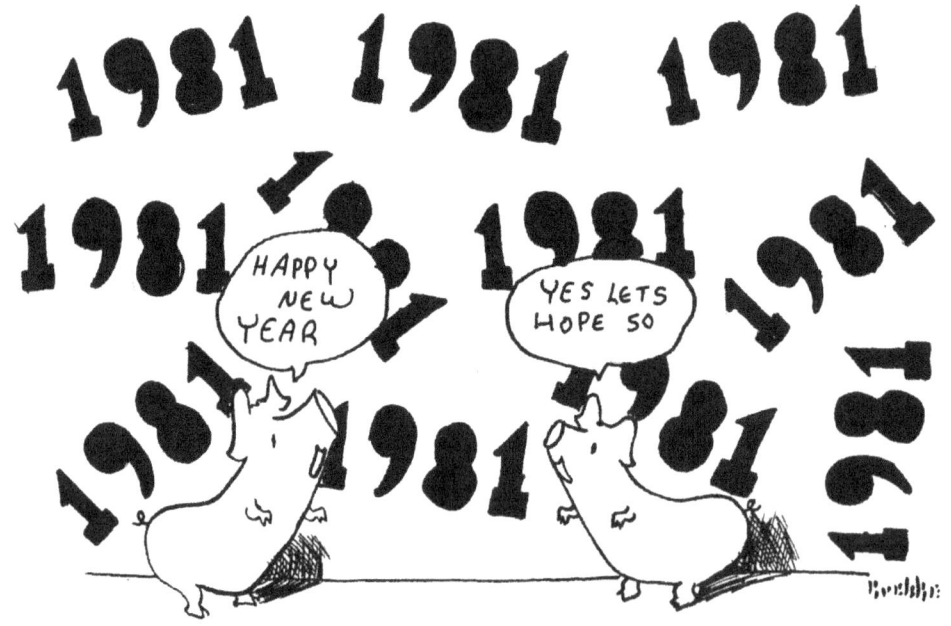

~ December 24, 1980

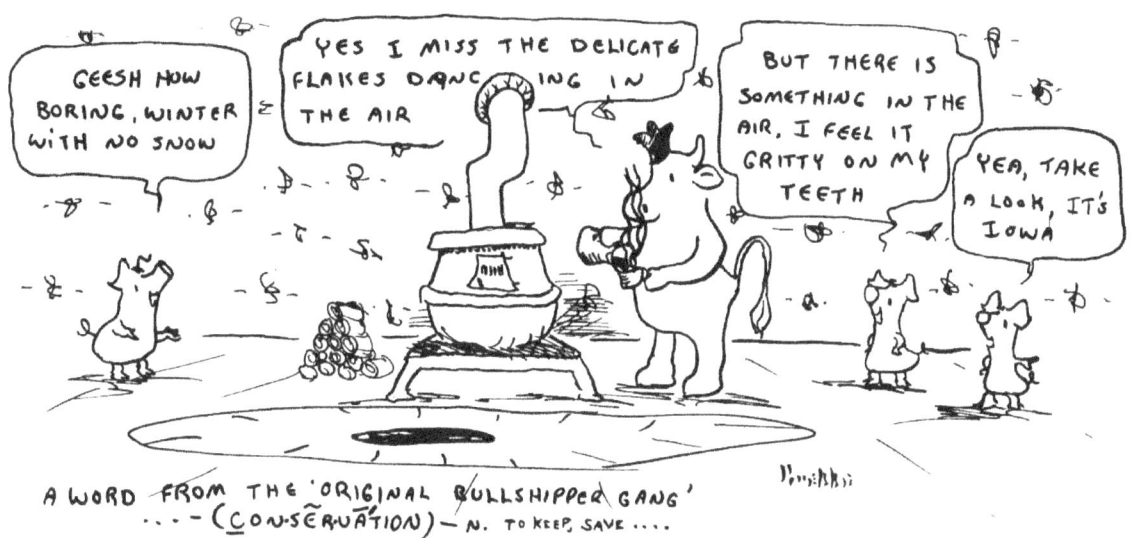

~ December 31, 1980

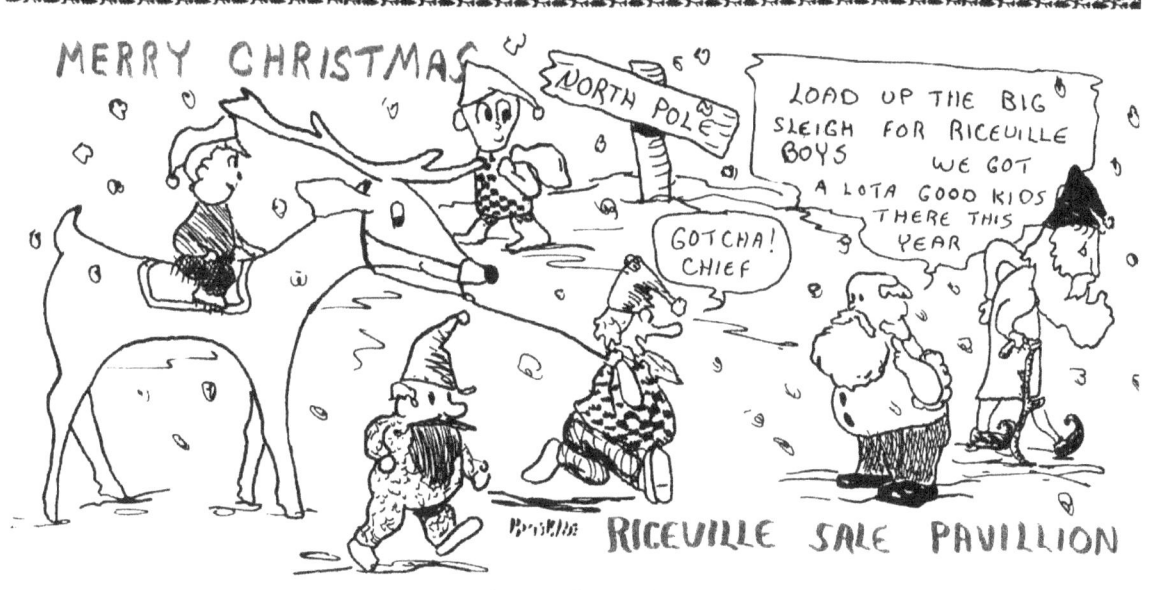

~ December, 1980

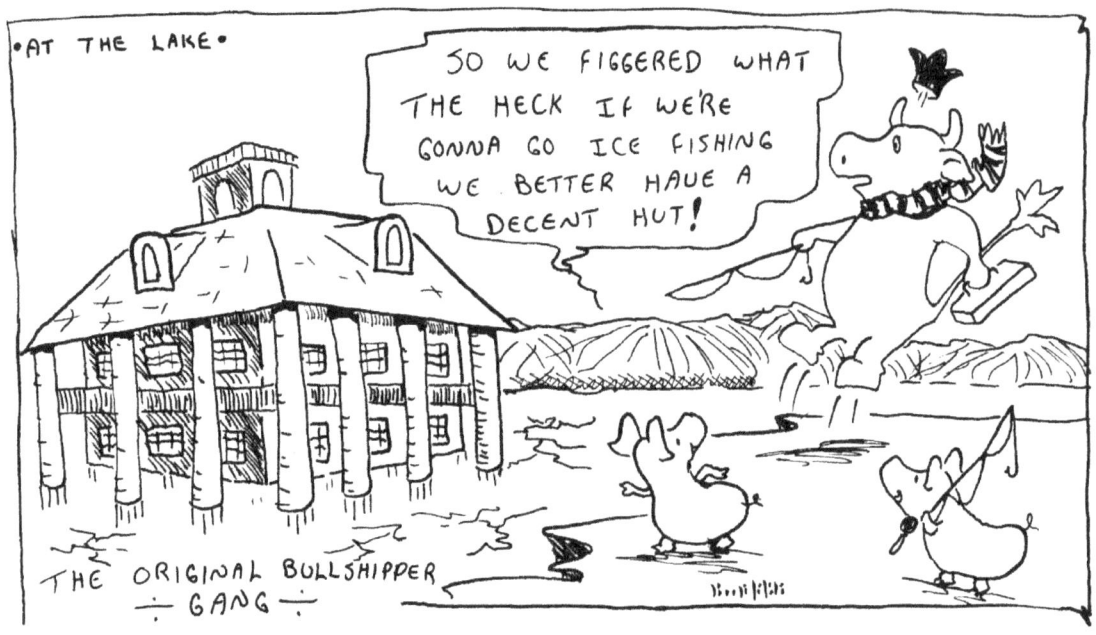

~ January 7, 14, 1981

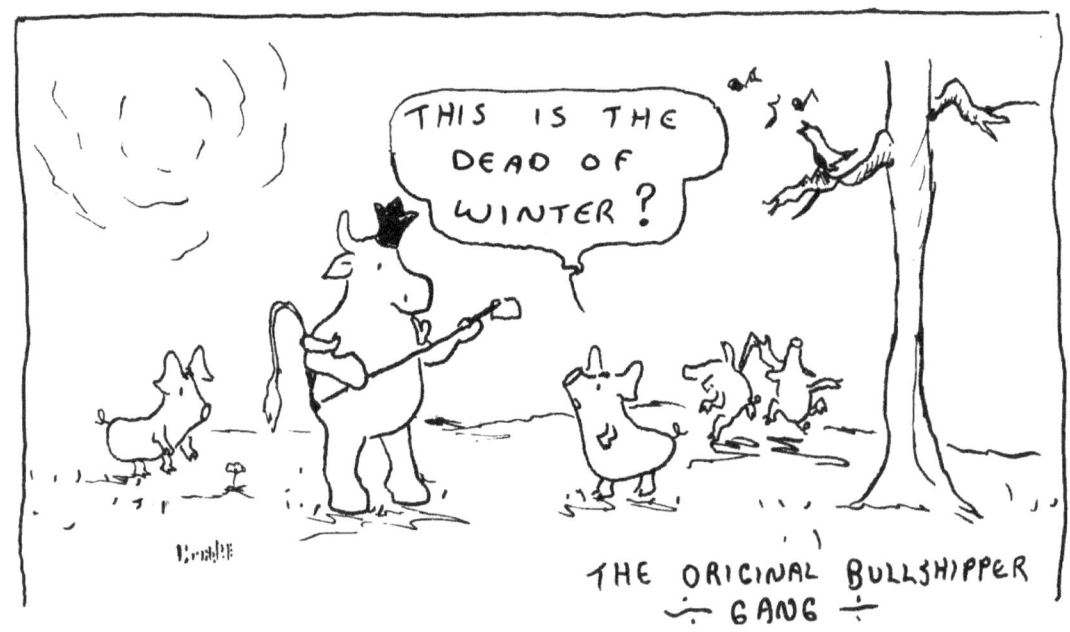

~ January 20, 1981

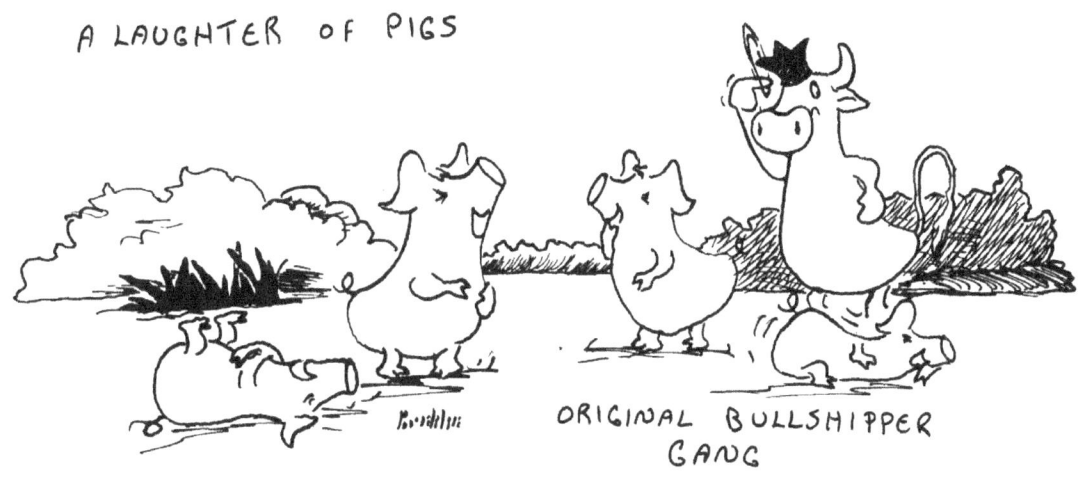

~ January 28, 1981

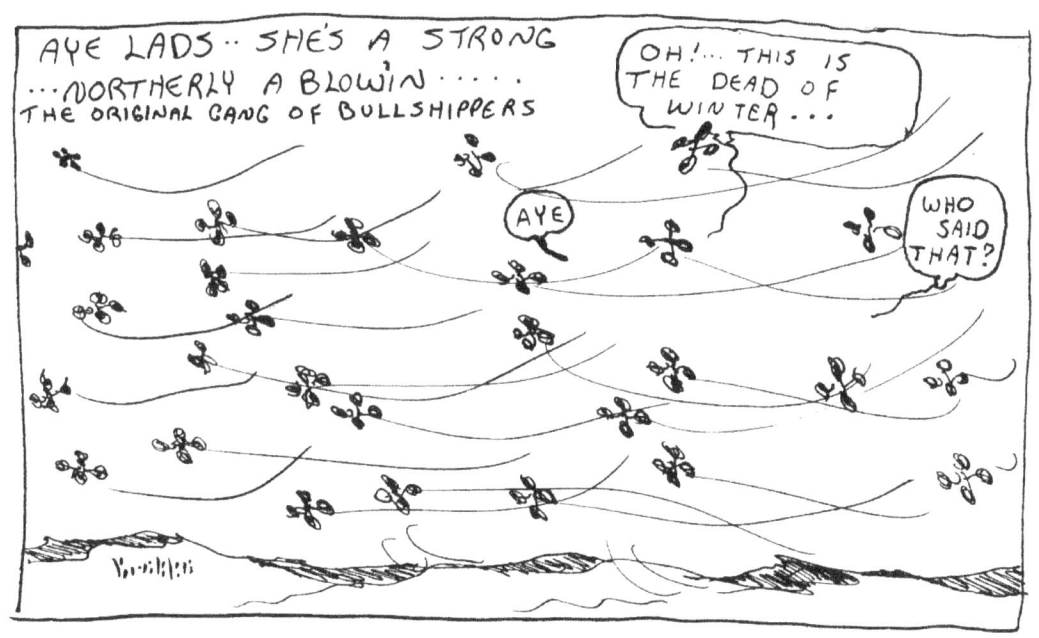

~ February 4, 1981

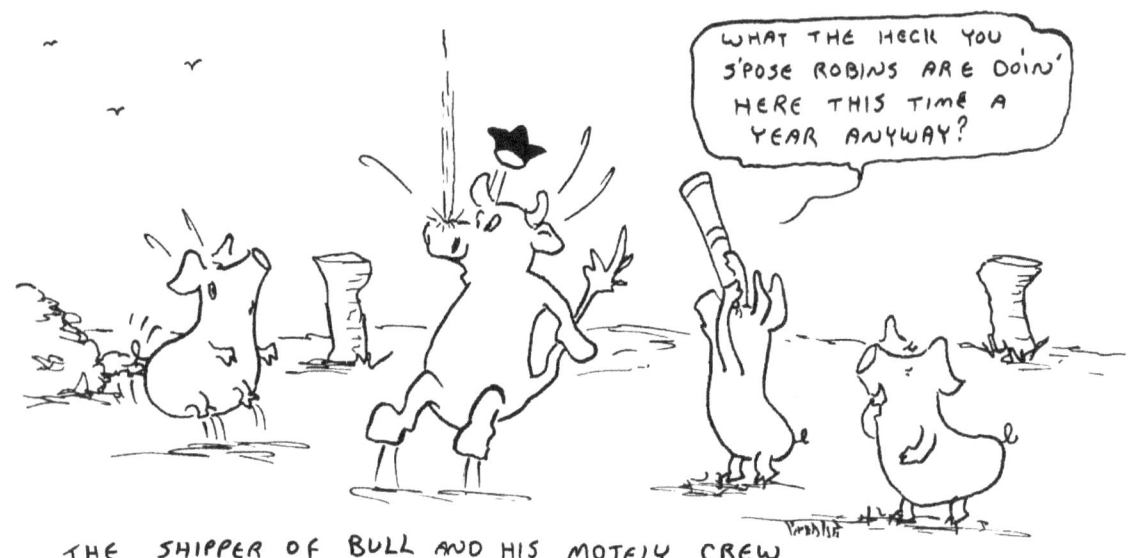

~ February 11, 1981

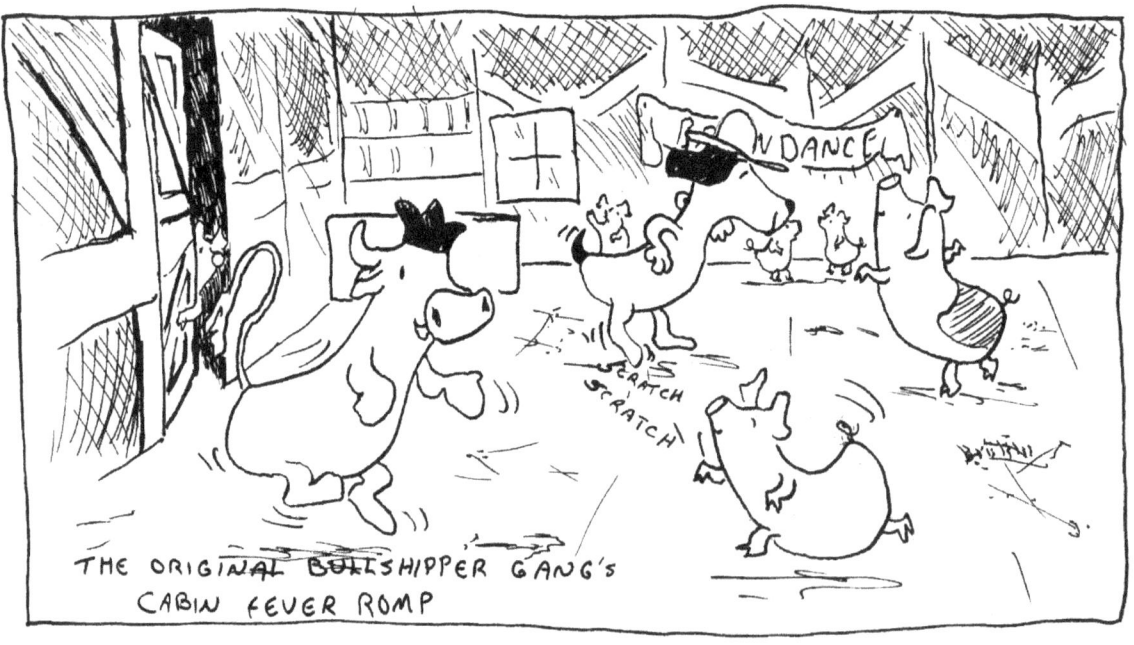

~ February 25, 1981

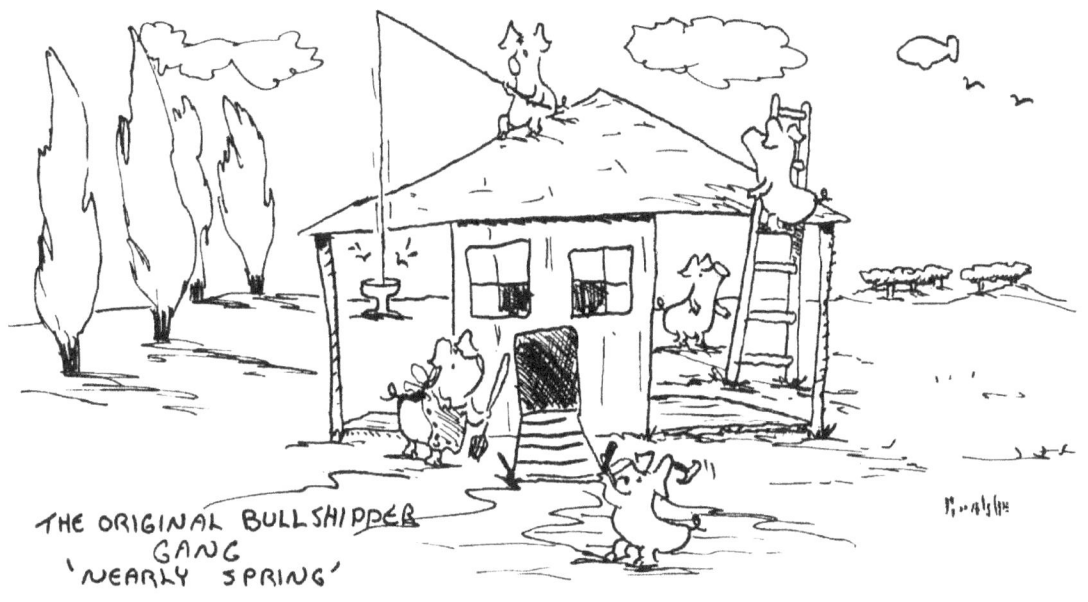

~ March 4, 1981

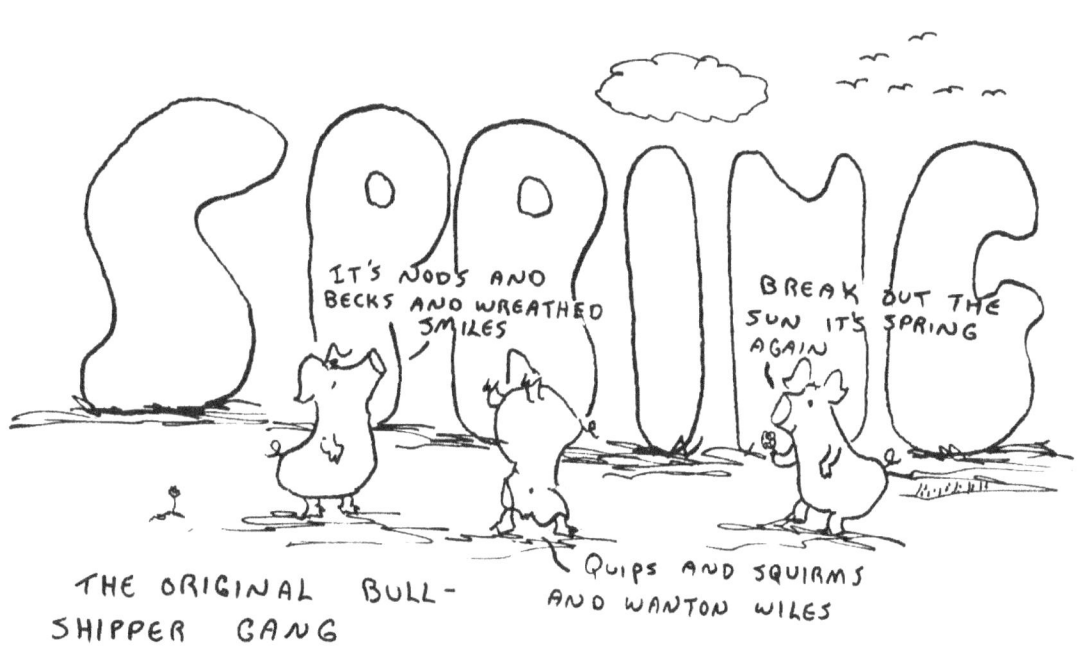

~ March 11, 1981

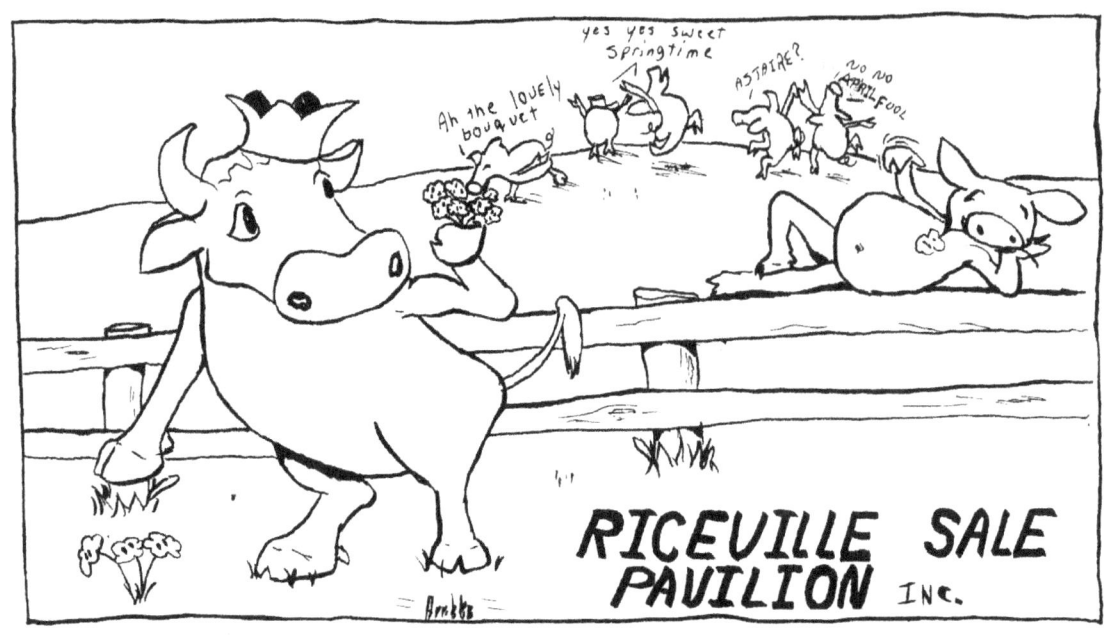

~ March 18, 25, 1981

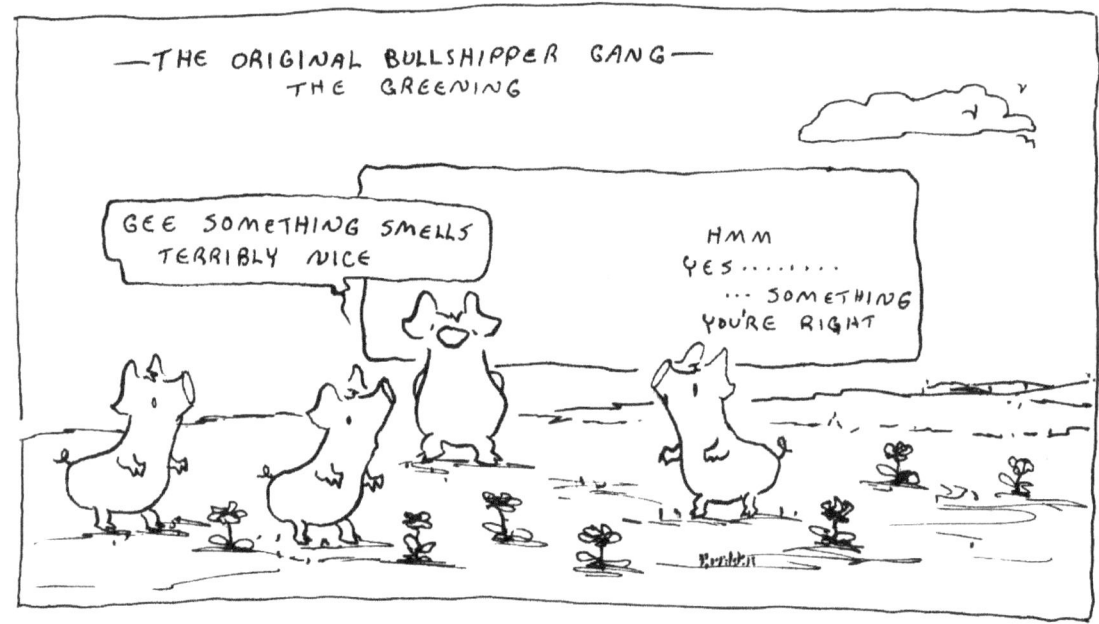

~ April 1, 8, 15, 1981

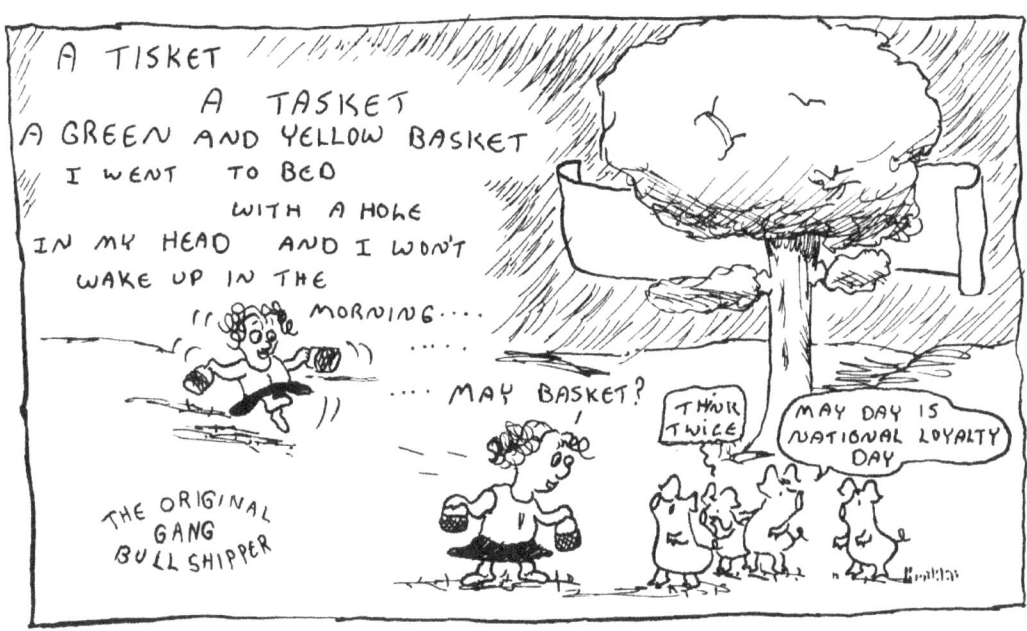

~ April 22, 1981

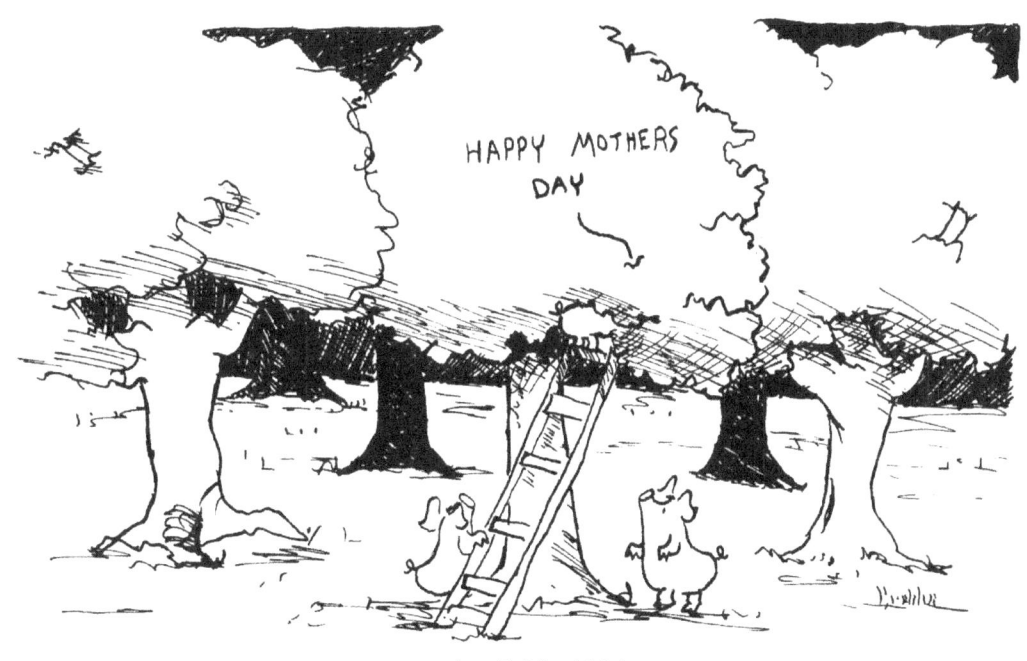

~ April 29, 1981

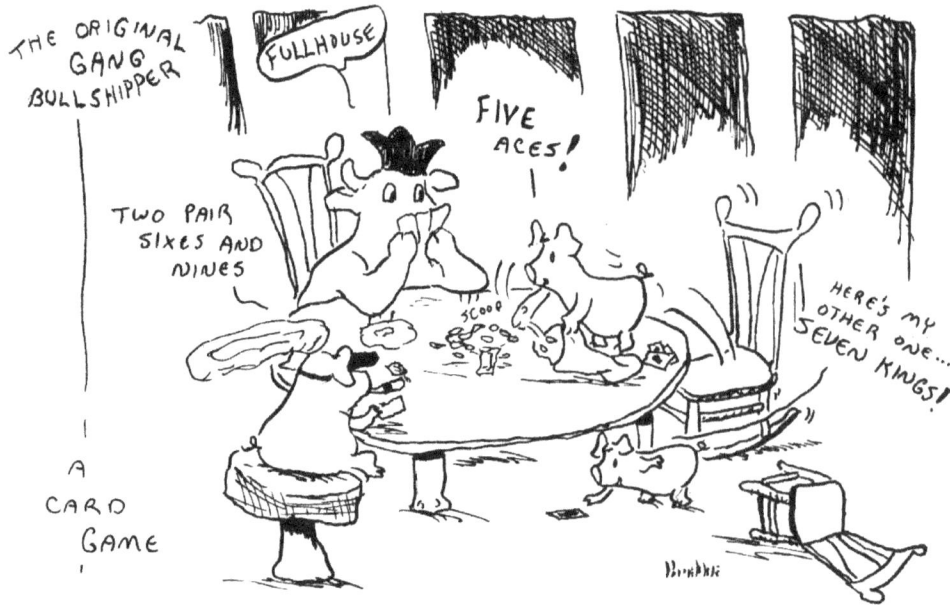

~ May 6, 1981

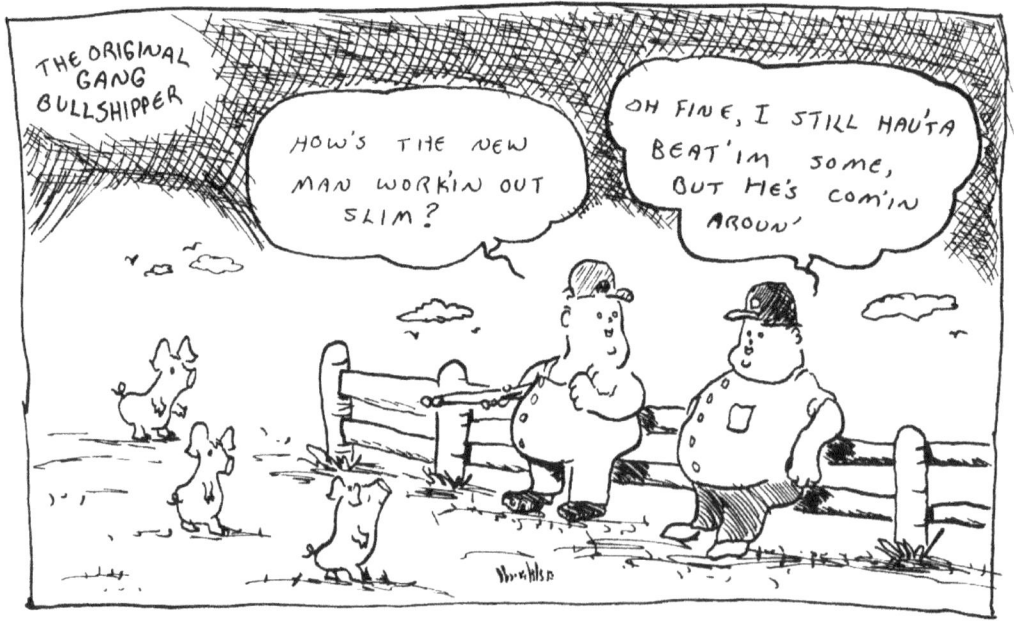

~ May 13, 1981

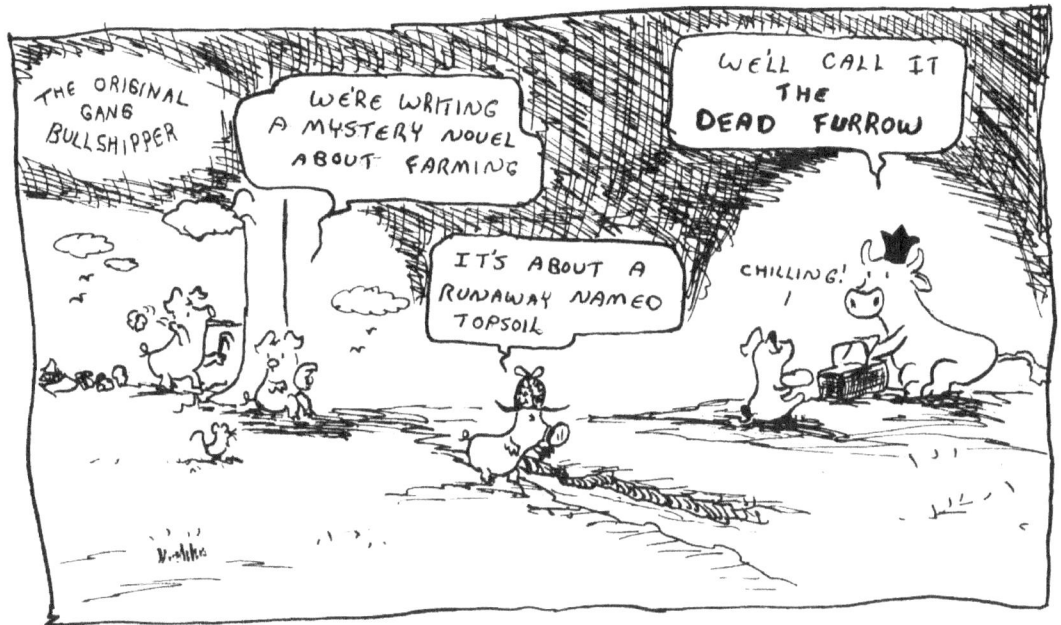

~ May 20, 1981

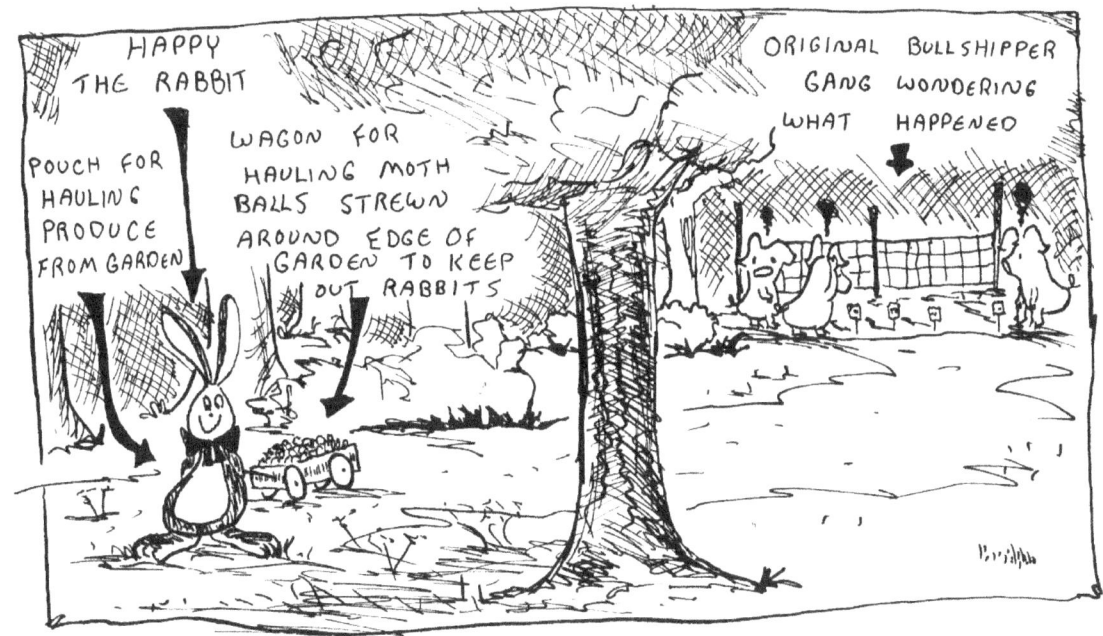

~ June 10, 1981

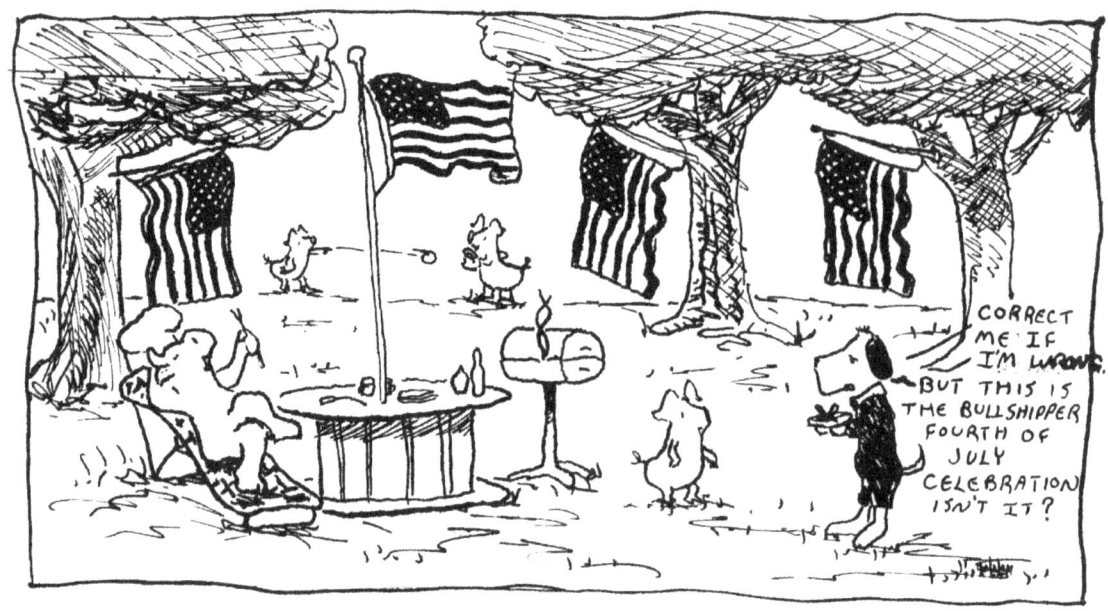

~ June 24, 1981

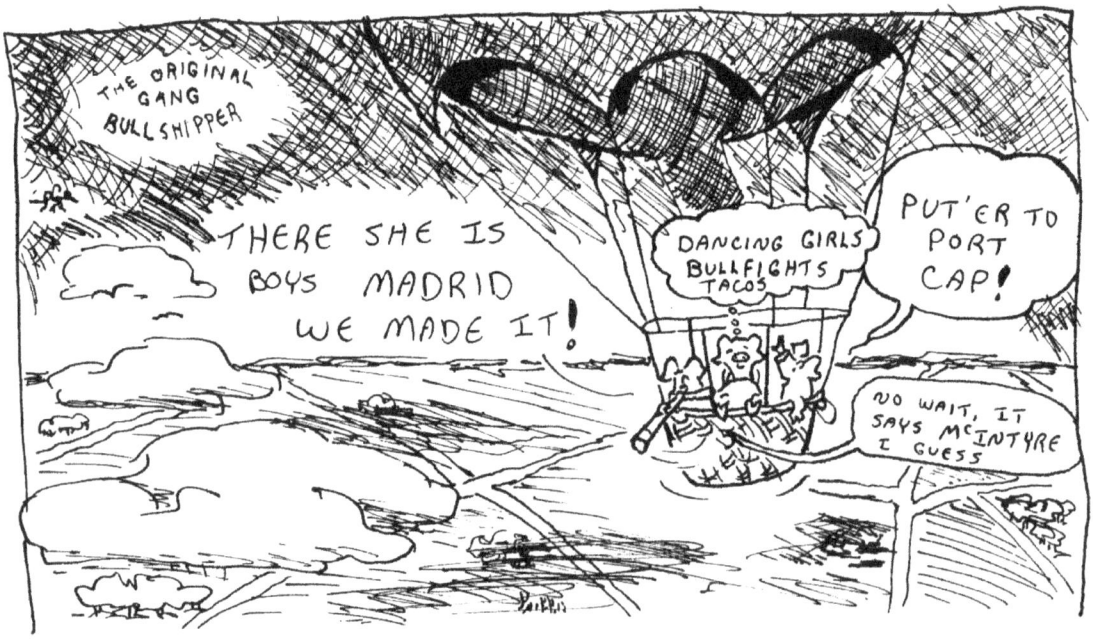

~ July 8, 15, 1981

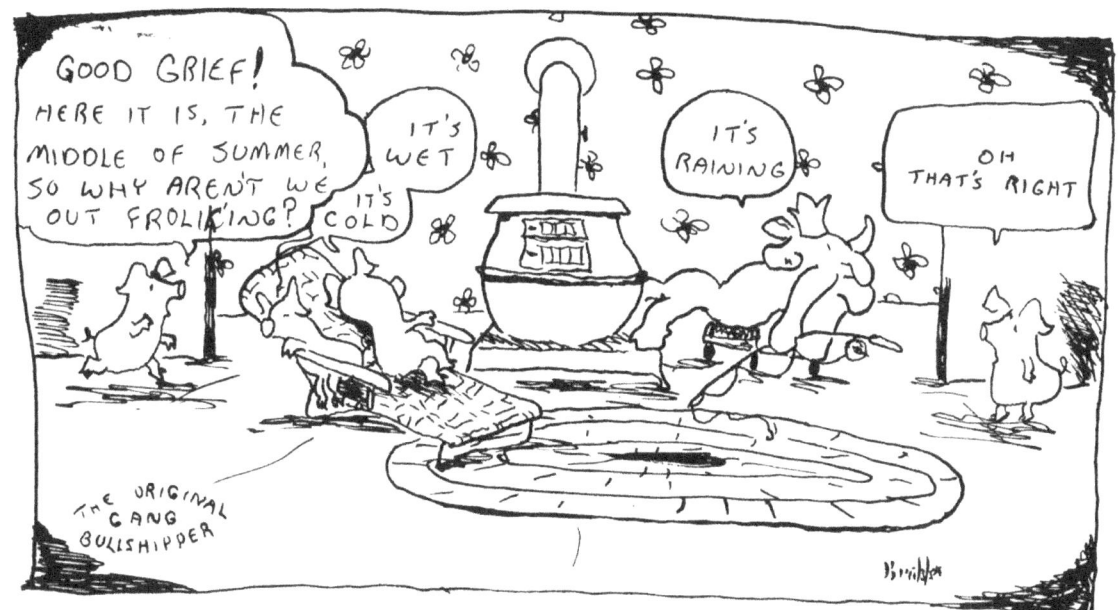

~ July 22, 1981

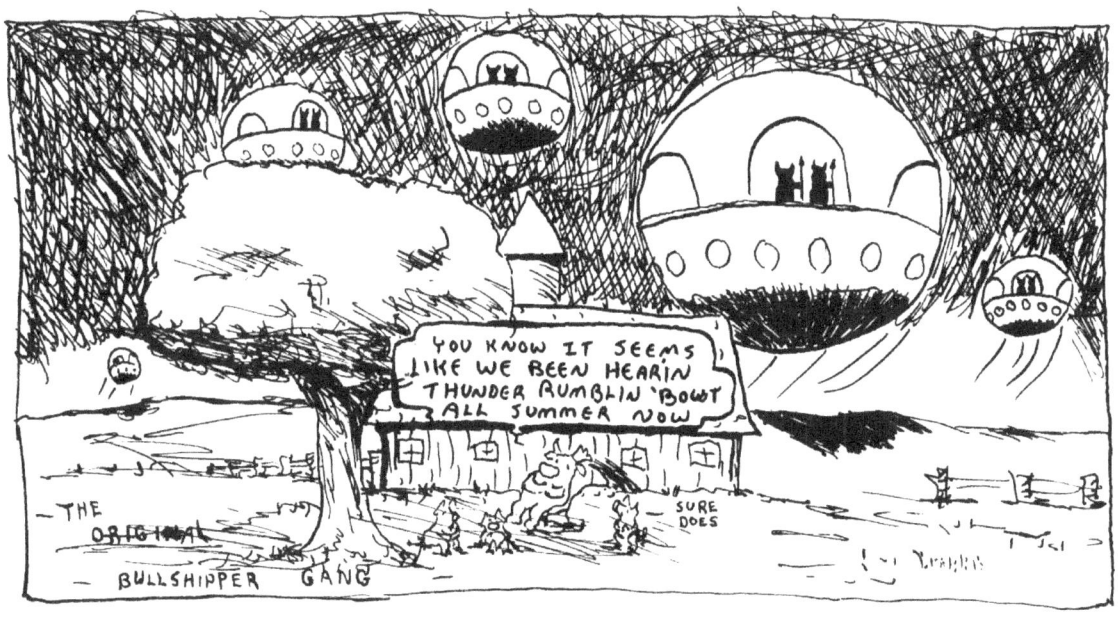

~ July 29, 1981

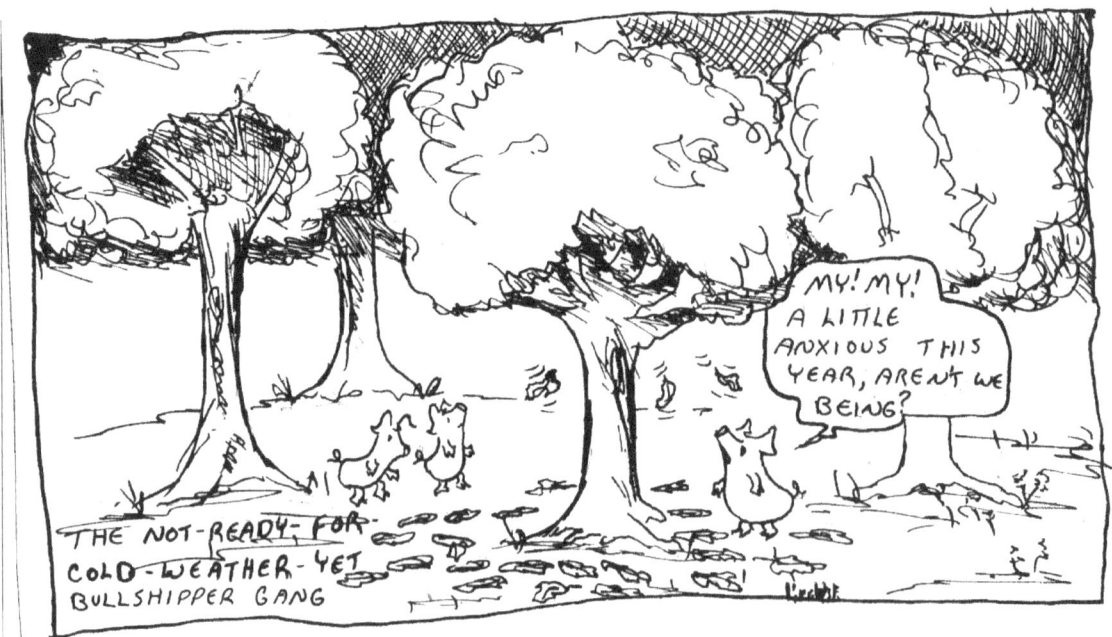

~ August 5, 19, 26, 1981

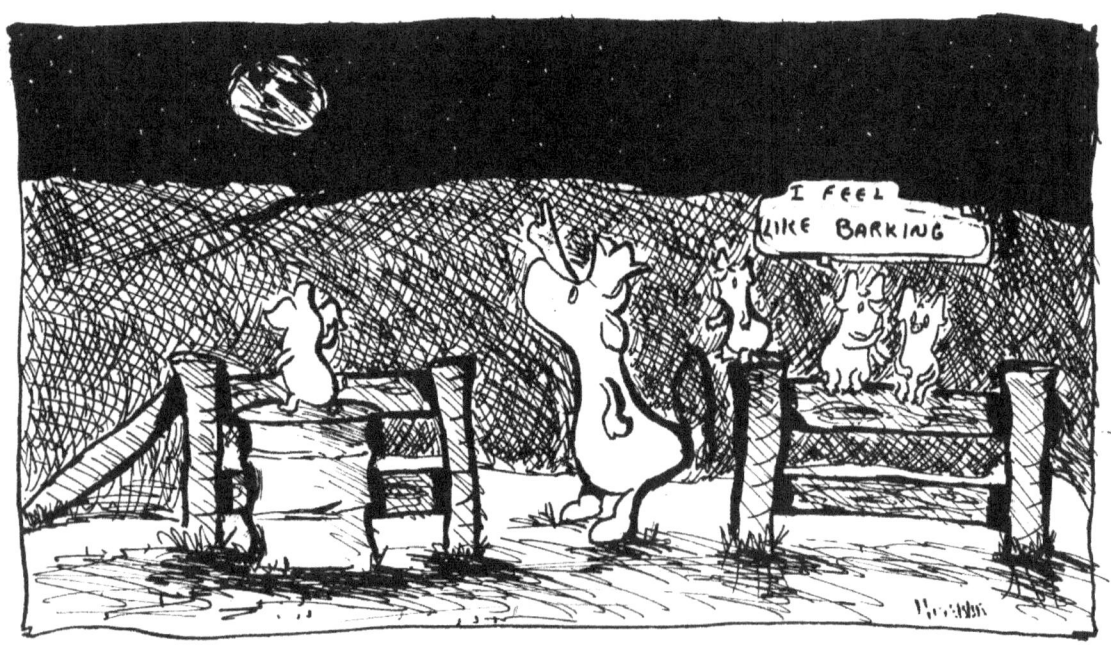

~ August 12, 1981

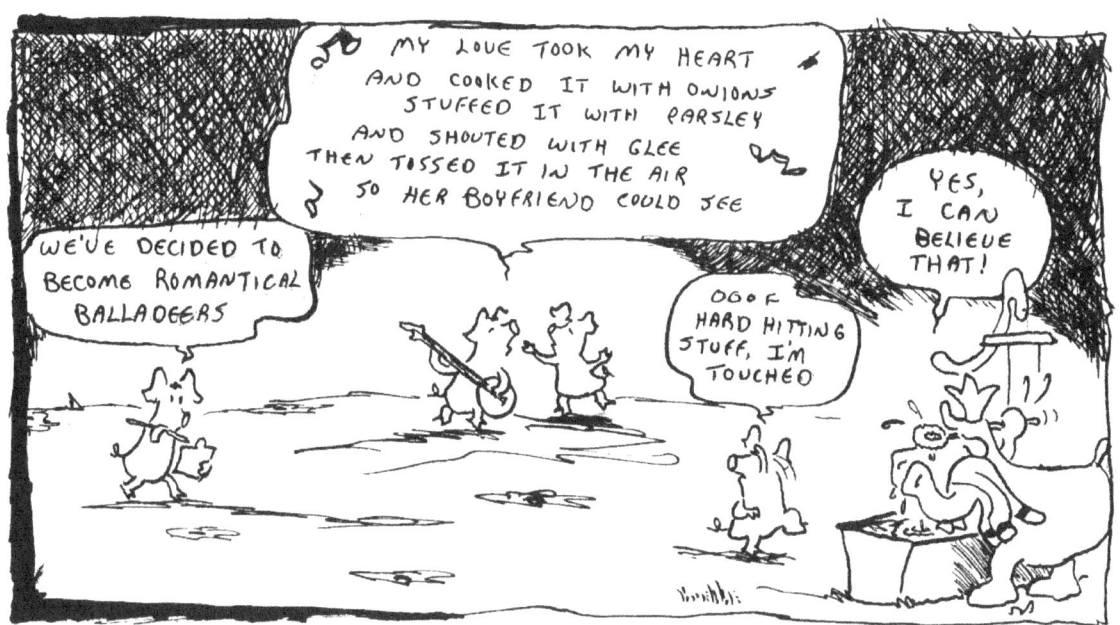

~ September 9, 1981

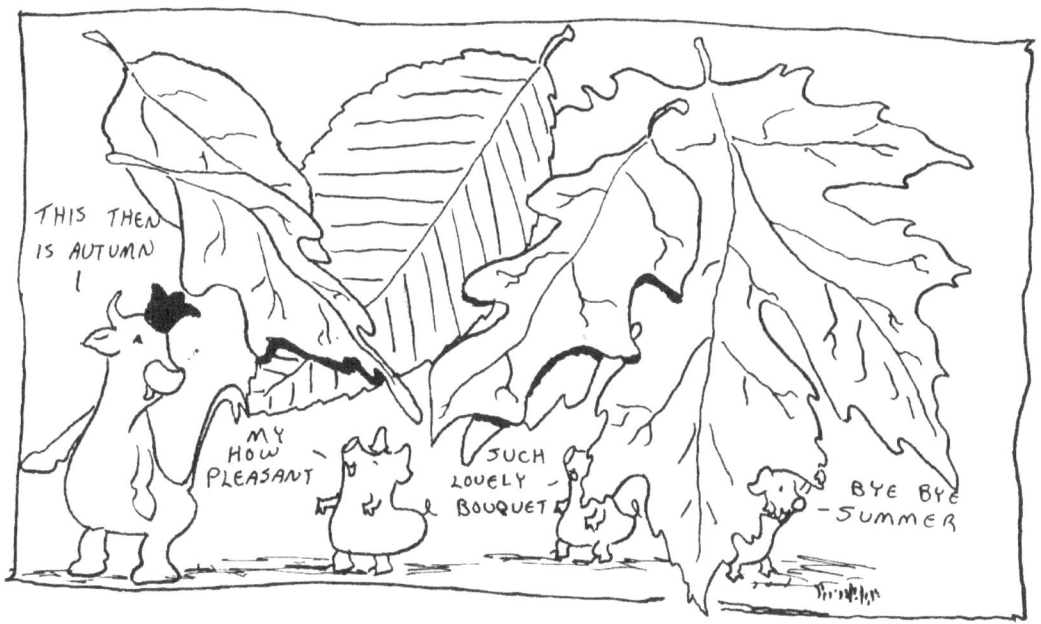

~ September 16, 1981

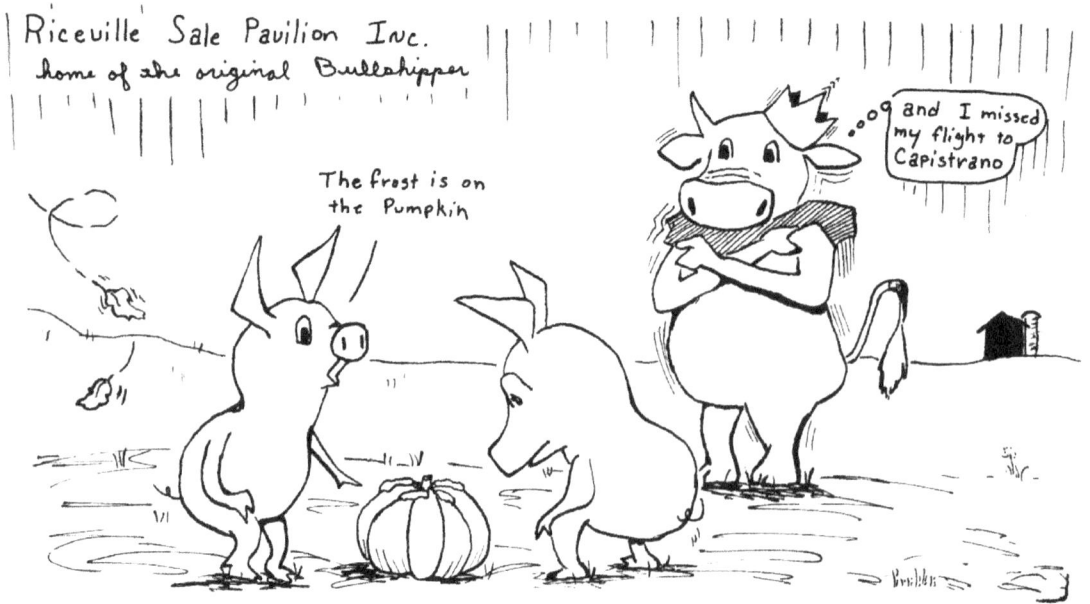

~ October 14, 21, 28, 1981

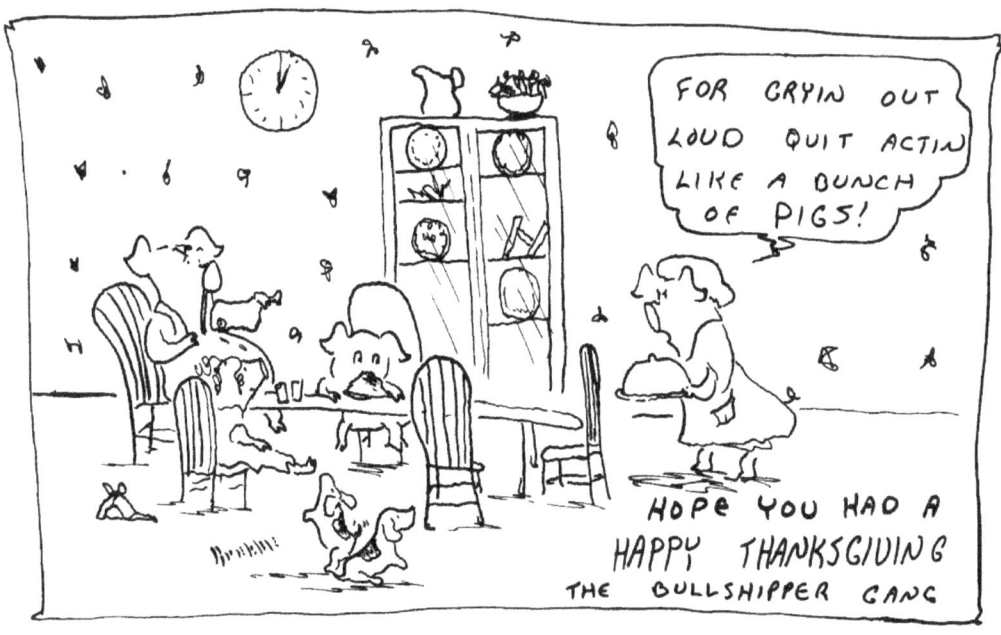

~ November 25 and December 2, 1981

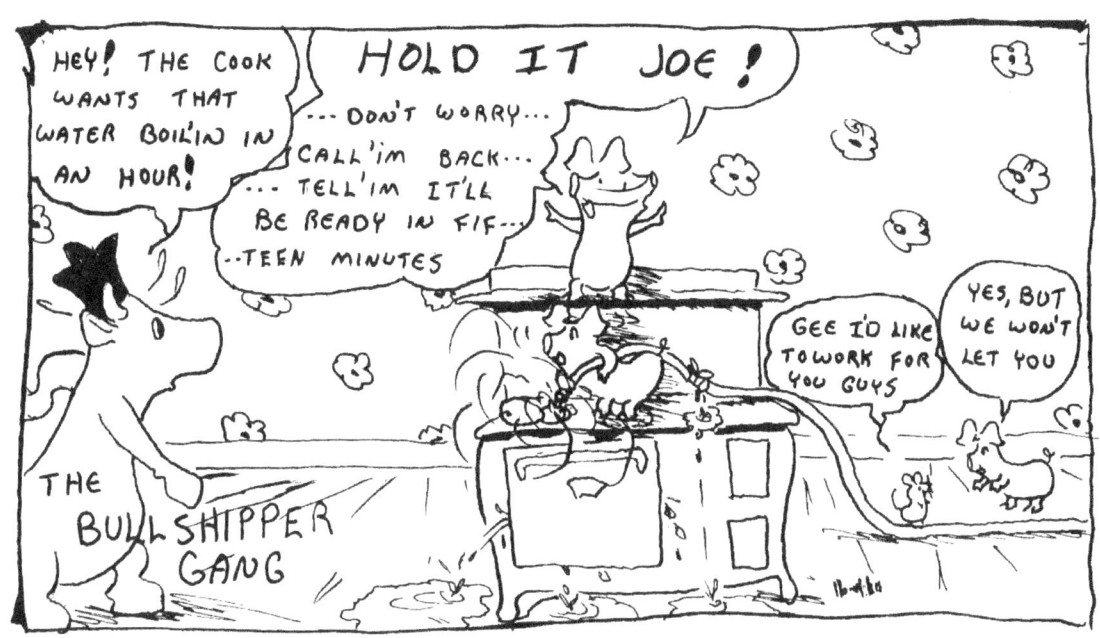

~ 1981

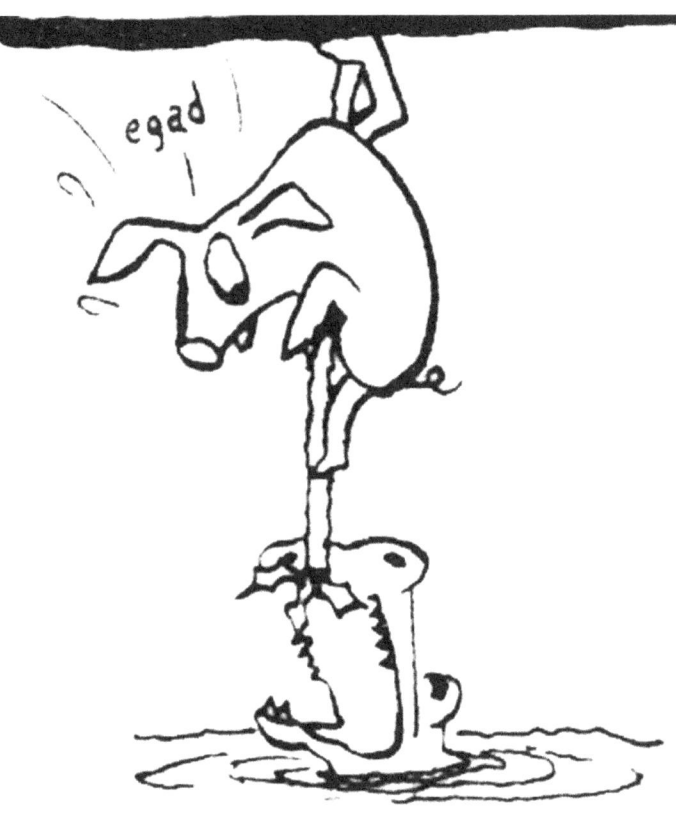

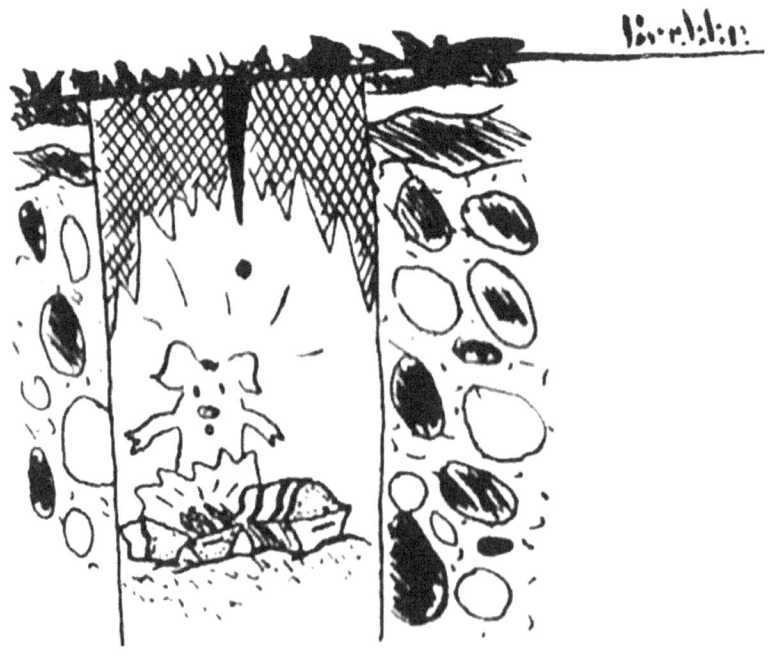

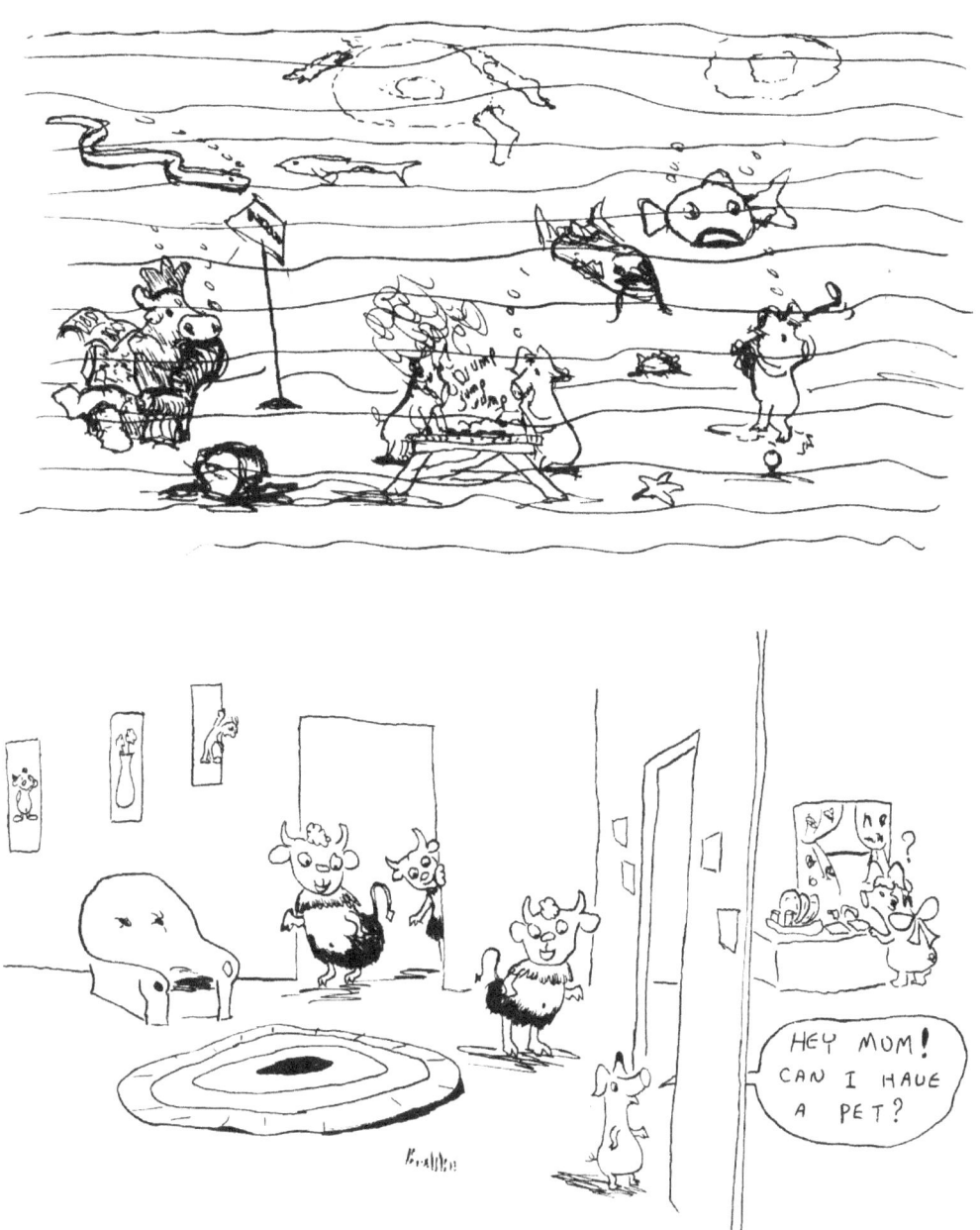

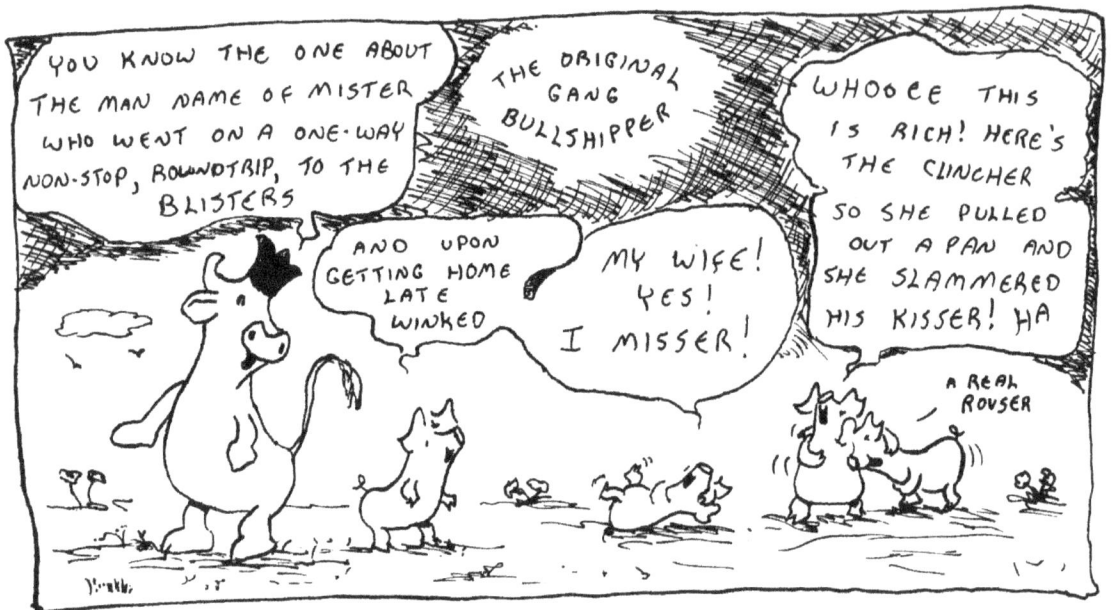

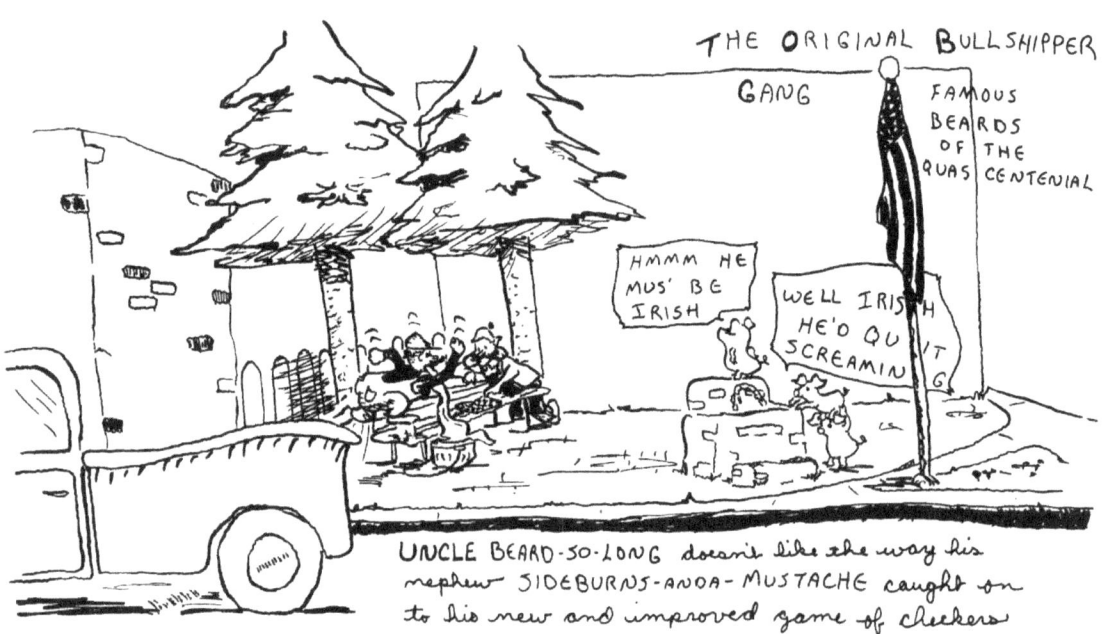

UNCLE BEARD-SO-LONG doesn't like the way his nephew SIDEBURNS-ANDA-MUSTACHE caught on to his new and improved game of checkers

www.ingramcontent.com/pod-product-compliance
Lightning Source LLC
Chambersburg PA
CBHW081609220526
45468CB00010B/2826